BRIGHT & Brainy

1st Grade Practice

Author

Suzanne Barchers, Ed.D.

SHELL EDUCATION

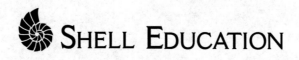

Publishing Credits

Dona Herweck Rice, *Editor-in-Chief*; Robin Erickson, *Production Director*;
Lee Aucoin, *Creative Director*; Timothy J. Bradley, *Illustration Manager*;
Sara Johnson, M.S.Ed, *Senior Editor*; Evelyn Garcia, *Associate Education Editor*;
Leah Quillian, *Assistant Editor*; Grace Alba, *Designer*;
Corinne Burton, M.A.Ed., *Publisher*

Shell Education

5301 Oceanus Drive
Huntington Beach, CA 92649-1030
http://www.shelleducation.com

ISBN 978-1-4258-0884-6

© 2012 Shell Educational Publishing, Inc.

Table of Contents

Every Child Is Bright and Brainy

The Need for Continual Practice

"Practice makes perfect."

That's what they say, and it's usually true! Although educational practices have changed over time, some key methods have stayed the same. Children need plenty of opportunity to practice skills and show what they know. The more they do, the more they can transfer their learning to everyday life—and future success!

Of course, there has to be a good purpose for the practice. That is where the pages in this book come in. Created with the essential standards in mind, each activity page focuses on a particular concept, skill, or skill-set and provides students abundant opportunities to practice and achieve mastery.

Annis and Annis (1987) found that continual repetition helps increase the levels of the Bloom cognitive domain. In other words, practice helps students learn in a wide variety of ways at all levels of cognitive ability. It provides students opportunities to think more deeply about the subjects they are studying. Marzano (2010) asserts that in order for students to independently display their learning, it is necessary for them to practice procedural skills. Providing students with ample opportunity to practice remains a key strategy for employing the best educational practices in or out of the classroom.

Every Child Is Bright and Brainy *(cont.)*

Understanding the Standards

The Common Core State Standards were developed in collaboration with a wide variety of educators through the Common Core State Standards Initiative. The goal was to create a clear and consistent framework to prepare students for higher education and the workforce. To this end, teachers, school administrators, and other educational experts worked together in a state-led effort coordinated by the National Governors Association Center for Best Practices (NGA) and the Council of Chief State School Officers (CCSSO).

The standards incorporate the most effective models from around the country and around the globe, providing teachers and parents with a shared understanding of what students are expected to learn. The consistency of the standards provides a common, appropriate benchmark for students unrelated to their location.

According to the NGA and the CCSSO, these standards meet the following criteria:

☼ They are aligned with college and work expectations;

☼ They are clear, understandable, and consistent;

☼ They include rigorous content and application of knowledge through high-order skills;

☼ They build upon strengths and lessons of current state standards;

☼ They are informed by other top-performing countries so that all students are prepared to succeed in our global economy and society; and

☼ They are evidence-based

Students who meet these standards within their K–12 education should have the skills and knowledge necessary to succeed in their educational careers and beyond.

Making It Work

It is important for you to understand the key features of this book, so that you can use it in a way that works for you and your students.

- **Standards-based practice.** The exercises in *Bright & Brainy: 1st Grade Practice* are aligned with the Common Core State Standards. Each activity page focuses on a particular concept, skill, or skill-set and provides students ample opportunities to practice and achieve mastery.

- **Clear, easy-to-understand activities.** The exercises in this book are written in a kid-friendly style.

- **Assessment of student progress.** Based on student progress, the Common Core State Standards Correlation Chart (pages 9–10) helps identify the grade-level standards with which students may need additional support.

- **Reinforcement of key grade-level concepts.** Each activity provides practice of key grade-level language arts and mathematics skills in an organized and meaningful way.

- **Stand-alone activity pages.** Each activity is flexible and can be used independently in a variety of instructional or at-home settings.

The chart below provides suggestions for how to implement the activities.

Whole/Small Group	Individual	At Home/Homework
• Read and discuss the directions at the beginning of each activity. Work practice problems on an interactive whiteboard, document camera, or other display method. • Have students work problems on the interactive whiteboard. • Have students take turns reading each question. • Display the problems and review and correct them. • Read and discuss responses.	• Create folders for each student. Include a copy of their selected activity pages. • Collect work and check student answers, or provide each student with copies of the answer key and allow them to check their own work. • Select specific activity pages to support individual students' needs for additional practice.	• Provide each student with activity pages to reinforce skills. • Collect work and check student answers, or provide each student with copies of the answer key and allow them to check their own work. • Select specific activity pages to provide extra support in areas where individual students may need additional practice.

Making It Work (cont.)

Bright & Brainy: 1st Grade Practice provides practice pages for a broad range of Common Core language arts and mathematics standards. Language arts topics are designed to provide students practice in the most vital skills included in the Common Core Standards. These range from reading foundational skills to fluency, and from writing to speaking and listening. Activities designed to support student learning of how to read informational texts, literature, and vocabulary skills round out the carefully chosen exercises. Within each of these broad areas are individual activity pages centering on subtopics, such as letter recognition, alike and different, antonyms, and rhyming. Each covered skill is crucial to achieving language fluency and to setting the stage for future success in language arts. Likewise, the chosen mathematics skills represent fundamental and integral topics from the Common Core Standards. Clear, student-friendly exercises center around the essential areas of counting and cardinal numbers, number and operations in base ten, operations and algebraic thinking, measuring, data, and geometry.

Individual lessons engage students in mastering specific skills, including more, less, same, sequencing, alike and different, and flat vs. solid.

This book covers the following:

- Reading: Foundational Skills
- Language Conventions
- Reading: Informational Text
- Vocabulary Acquisition and Use
- Reading: Literature
- Fluency

- Writing
- Speaking and Listening
- Number and Operations in Base Ten
- Operations and Algebraic Thinking
- Measurement and Data
- Geometry

Additionally, the Resource CD allows for easy access to the student activity pages in this book. Electronic PDF files of all the activity pages are included on the CD.

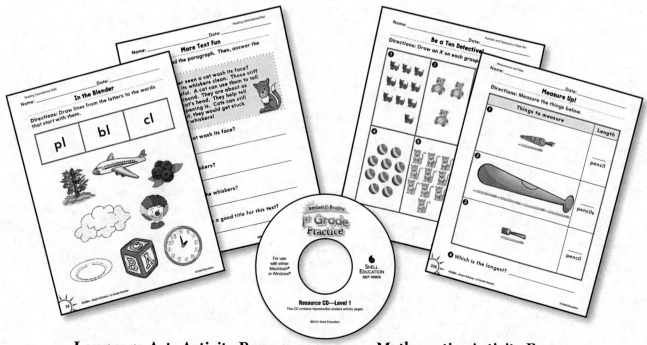

Language Arts Activity Pages   **Mathematics Activity Pages**

Correlation to Standards

Shell Education is committed to producing educational materials that are research and standards based. In this effort, we have correlated all of our products to the academic standards of all 50 United States, the District of Columbia, the Department of Defense Dependent Schools, and all Canadian provinces. We have also correlated to the Common Core State Standards.

How to Find Standards Correlations

To print a customized correlation report of this product for your state, visit our website at **http://www.shelleducation.com** and follow the on-screen directions. If you require assistance in printing correlation reports, please contact Customer Service at 1-800-858-7339.

Purpose and Intent of Standards

Legislation mandates that all states adopt academic standards that identify the skills students will learn in kindergarten through grade twelve. Many states also have standards for Pre-K. This same legislation sets requirements to ensure the standards are detailed and comprehensive.

Standards are designed to focus instruction and guide adoption of curricula. Standards are statements that describe the criteria necessary for students to meet specific academic goals. They define the knowledge, skills, and content students should acquire at each level. Standards are also used to develop standardized tests to evaluate students' academic progress.

Teachers are required to demonstrate how their lessons meet state standards. State standards are used in development of all of our products, so educators can be assured they meet the academic requirements of each state.

Common Core State Standards

The lessons in this book are aligned to the Common Core State Standards (CCSS). The standards listed on pages 9–10 support the objectives presented throughout the lessons.

Common Core State Standards Correlation Chart

Language Arts	
Reading: Foundational Skills	**Page(s)**
RF.1.1—Recognize the distinguishing features of a sentence	11–12
RF.1.2—Distinguish long from short vowel sounds	13–22
RF.1.2—Orally produce single-syllable words by blending sounds	23–27
RF.1.2—Isolate and pronounce initial, medial vowel, and final sounds	28–31
RF.1.3—Know the spelling-sound correspondences for common consonant digraphs	32–35
RF.1.3—Decode regularly spelled one-syllable words	36–37
RF.1.3—Know common vowel team conventions for representing long vowel sounds	38–39
RF.1.3—Decode words following basic patterns by breaking the words into syllables	40–44
RF.1.3—Read words with inflectional endings	45–46
RF.1.3—Recognize and read grade-appropriate irregularly spelled words	47–49
Language Conventions	**Page(s)**
L.1.1—Print all upper- and lowercase letters	50–53
L.1.1—Use common, proper, and possessive nouns	54–56
L.1.1—Use singular and plural nouns with matching verbs in basic sentences	57–59
L.1.1—Use personal, possessive, and indefinite pronouns	60–62
L.1.1—Use verbs to convey a sense of past, present, and future	63–65
L.1.1—Use frequently occuring conjunctions	66–68
L.1.1—Use frequently occuring adjectives	69–71
L.1.1—Use determiners	72–74
L.1.1—Use frequently occuring prepositions	75–77
L.1.1—Produce and expand complete simple and compound declarative, interrogative, imperative, and exclamatory sentences in response to prompts	78–81
L.1.2—Capitalize dates and names of people	82–83
L.1.2—Use end punctuation for sentences	84–86
L.1.2—Use commas in dates and to separate single words in a series	87–89
L.1.2—Spell untaught words phonetically, drawing on phonemic awareness and spelling conventions	90–91
Reading: Informational Text	**Page(s)**
R1.1.1—Ask and answer questions about key details in a text	92–95
R1.1.2—Identify the main topic and retell key details of a text	96–99
R1.1.5—Know and use various text features to locate key facts or information in a text	100–101
R1.1.7—Use the illustrations and details in a text to describe its key ideas	102–105, 108–110
R1.1.8—Identify the reasons an author gives to support points in a text	106–107
Vocabulary Acquisition and Use	**Page(s)**
L.1.4—Determine or clarify the meaning of unknown and multiple-meaning words and phrases	111–115
L.1.5—With guidance and support from adults, demonstrate understanding of figurative language, word relationships and nuances in word meanings	116–127
Reading: Literature	**Page(s)**
RL.1.1—Ask and answer questions about key details in a text	128–135
RL.1.2–1.10—Retell stories, including key details, and demonstrate understanding of their central message or lesson	136–137

Common Core State Standards
Correlation Chart *(cont.)*

Language Arts *(cont.)*	
Fluency	**Page(s)**
RF.1.4—Read with sufficient accuracy and fluency to support comprehension	138–139
Writing	**Page(s)**
W.1.1—Write opinion pieces in which they introduce the topic or name the book they are writing about, state an opinion, supply a reason for the opinion, and provide some sense of closure	140–142
W.1.2—Write informative/explanatory texts in which they name a topic, supply some facts about the topic, and provide some sense of closure	143
W.1.3—Write narratives in which they recount two or more appropriately sequenced events	144–146
W.1.7—Participate in shared research and writing projects	147–152
Speaking and Listening	**Page(s)**
Sl.1.1–6—Participate in collaborative conversations with diverse partners	153–154
Mathematics	
Number and Operations in Base Ten	**Page(s)**
1.NBT.1—Count to 120, starting at any number less than 120	155–158
1.NBT.2—Understand that the two digits of a two-digit number represent amounts of tens and ones	159–168
1.NBT.3—Compare two two-digit numbers based on meanings of the tens and ones digits	169–173
1.NBT.4—Add within 100, including adding a two-digit number and a one-digit number, and adding a two-digit number and a multiple of 10	174–182
1.NBT.5—Given a two-digit number, mentally find 10 more or 10 less	183–184
1.NBT.6—Subtract multiples of 10 in the range 10–90 from multiples of 10 in the range 10–90	185–190
Operations and Algebraic Thinking	**Page(s)**
1.OA.1—Use addition and subtraction within 20 to solve word problems	191–194
1.OA.2—Solve word problems that call for addition of three whole numbers	195–196
1.OA.3—Apply properties of operations as strategies to add and subtract	197
1.OA.4—Understand subtraction as an unknown-addend problem	198–199
1.OA.5—Relate counting to addition and subtraction	200–203
1.OA.8—Determine the unknown whole number in an addition or subtraction equation relating three whole numbers	204–207
Measurement and Data	**Page(s)**
1.MD.1—Order three objects by length; compare the lengths of two objects	209, 211
1.MD.2—Express the length of an object as a whole number of length units	208, 210
1.MD.3—Tell and write time in hours and half-hours	212–214
1.MD.4—Organize, represent, and interpret data with up to three categories	215–217
Geometry	**Page(s)**
1.G.1—Distinguish between defining attributes	218–221, 229–230
1.G.2—Compose two-dimensional shapes	222–223, 225, 227
1.G.3—Partition circles and rectangles into two and four equal shares	231–233

Name: _____ Date: _____

Which Word Is Right?

Directions: Choose the right word for each sentence.

1 _____My_____ name is Jane.

⬭My⬭   my

2 _____Do_____ you know how to ride a bike?

(Do)   do

3 _____I_____ like to ride in the bike lane.

i   (I)

4 _____there_____ are no cars in the bike lane.

there   (There)

5 _____Dad_____ says I am a good rider!

(Dad)   dad

Name: _____ **Date:** _____

Finish It!

Directions: Choose the best punctuation for each sentence.

1 I went walking with my dog_____._____

                   !

2 Do you have a dog _____

       !   ?

3 My dog is kind _____

       .   ?

4 One time she got away _____

       .   ?

5 I was so worried _____

       ?   !

Name: _____ Date: _____

Name That Sound

Directions: Draw a circle around the pictures with short vowel sounds.

Name: _____ **Date:** _____

Name More Sounds

. . . .

Directions: Draw a circle around the pictures with short vowel sounds.

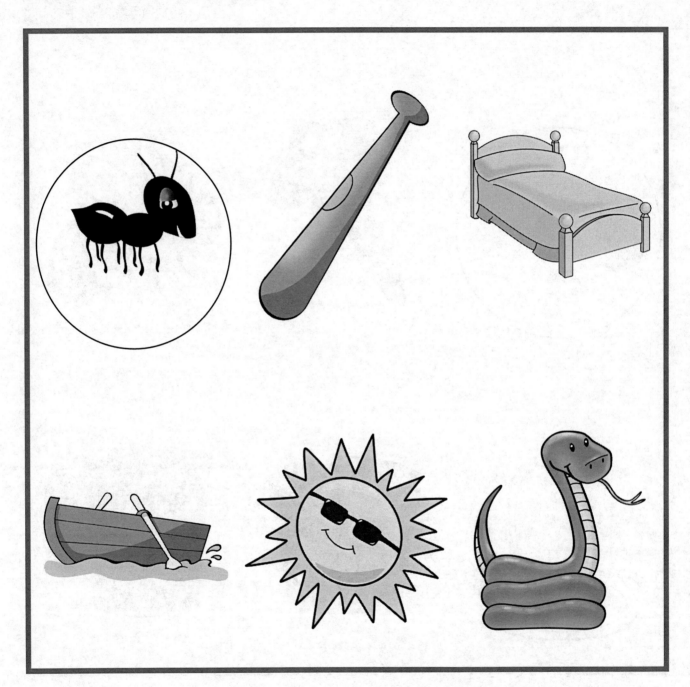

Name: _____ Date: _____

Pan or Pane?

Directions: Write the correct word in each blank.

1 Put the egg in the _____ pan _____ .

(pan)   pane

2 Dad put the bag in the _____ .

vane   van

3 _____ likes to ride his bike.

Tim   Time

4 Bob will _____ up.

mop   mope

5 Do _____ go yet.

not   note

Name: _____ Date: _____

In the Tub or Tube?

Directions: Write the correct word in each blank.

1 Put the toys in the _____.

(tub)   tube

2 The kid _____ into the apple.

bite   bit

3 I _____ down the hill.

slide   slid

4 The baby took a _____.

nap   nape

5 The bear _____ is black.

cub   cube

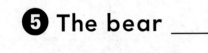

Name: _____ Date: _____

Find the Long Sounds

Directions: Draw a circle around the pictures with long vowel sounds.

Name: _____ **Date:** _____

More Long Sounds

. . . .

Directions: Draw a circle around the pictures with long vowel sounds.

Name: _____ Date: _____

Kit or Kite?

Directions: Write the correct word in each blank.

1 I like to fly my _____ kite _____.

      (kite)   kit

2 I can fix the paper with _____.

       tap   tape

3 Put on a _____.

       robe   rob

4 I _____ up the big hill.

       rod   rode

5 The hill has a big _____.

       slop   slope

Name: _____ **Date:** _____

Hop or Hope?

....

Directions: Write the correct word in the blank.

1 I _____hope_____ I get to go.

hop   ⬭hope⬯

2 The apple is _____.

rip   ripe

3 The _____ tree is green.

pine   pin

4 Rake the leaves into a _____.

pill   pile

5 I _____ you a book.

made   mad

Name: _____ Date: _____

Vowel Sound Match

Directions: Does the underlined word have a short vowel sound or a long vowel sound? Circle your answer.

1 Do not __poke__ the bear.

short   (long)

2 Put the tool __kit__ here.

short   long

3 He ran to home __base__.

short   long

4 May I have some __tape__?

short   long

5 He wore a __cap__.

short   long

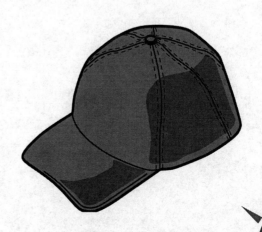

Name: _____ Date: _____

More Vowel Sound Matches

Directions: Draw a line from the underlined short vowel word to the word *short*. Draw a line from the long vowel word to the word *long*.

1 __Jan__ gave the bag to __Jane__.

short   long

2 The pilot has a __plan__ for the __plane__.

short   long

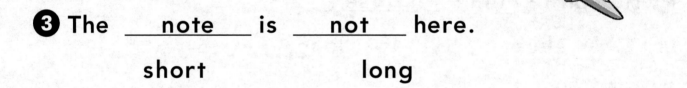

3 The __note__ is __not__ here.

short   long

4 The __pin__ is under the __pine__ tree.

short   long

5 The __pan__ is by the __pane__ of glass.

short   long

#50884—Bright & Brainy: 1st Grade Practice   © Shell Education

Name: _____ Date: _____

Beginning to Blend

Directions: Draw lines from the letters to the words that start with them.

br	dr	gr

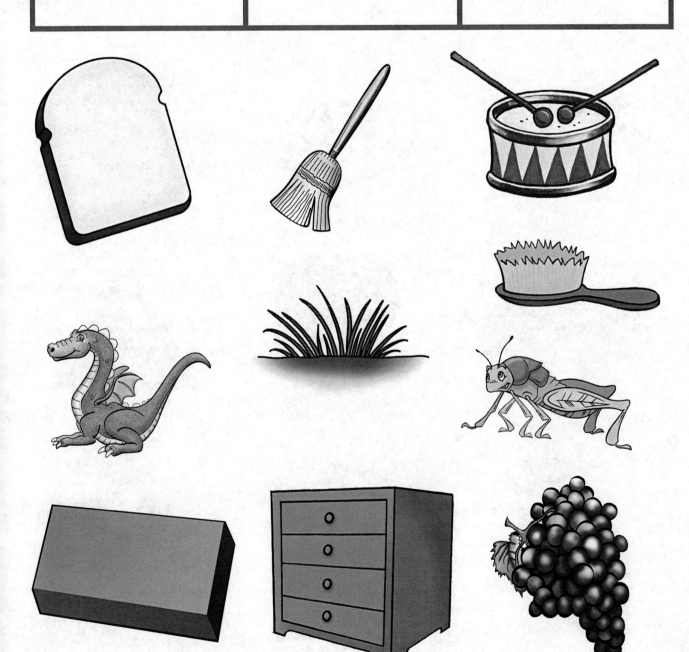

Name: _____ Date: _____

Which Blend Is It?

Directions: Draw lines from the letters to the words that start with them.

cr	pr	tr

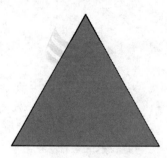

Name: _____ **Date:** _____

Choose the Blend

Directions: Draw lines from the letters to the words that start with them.

fr	gl	fl

Name: _____ **Date:** _____

In the Blender

Directions: Draw lines from the letters to the words that start with them.

pl	bl	cl

Name: _____ **Date:** _____

Blend Some More

Directions: Draw lines from the letters to the words that start with them.

sk	sp	st

Name: _____ Date: _____

What Is That Short Vowel?

Directions: Write the letter of the vowel in each word on the line under the picture.

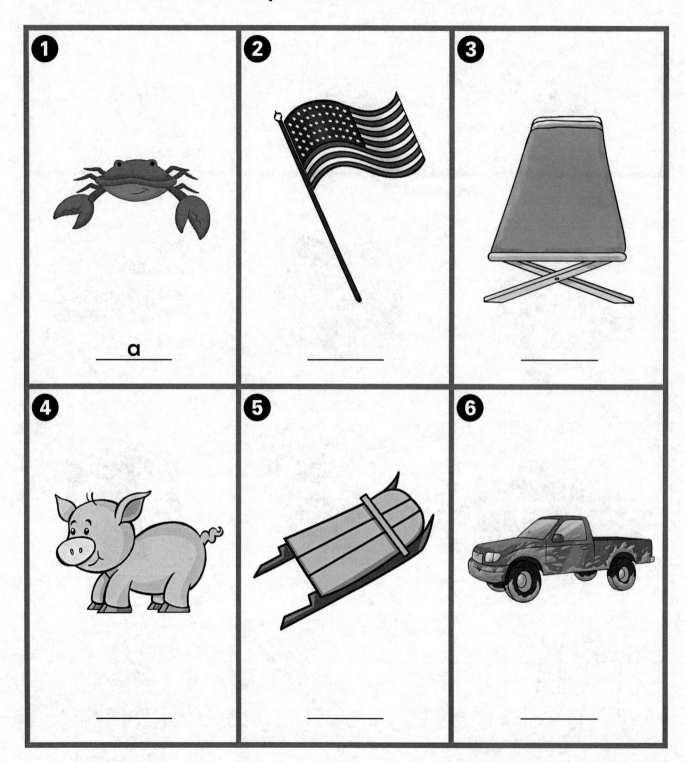

1   a

2   _____

3   _____

4   _____

5   _____

6   _____

Name: _____ Date: _____

What Is That Long Vowel?

Directions: Write the letter of the vowel in each word on the line under the picture.

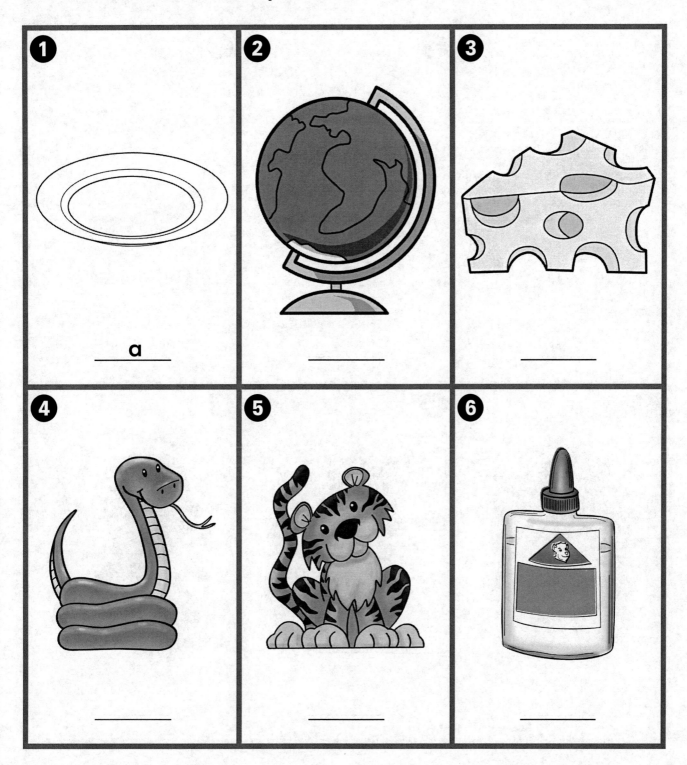

① ____a____

② _____

③ _____

④ _____

⑤ _____

⑥ _____

Name: _____ Date: _____

What Is That Final Sound?

Directions: Write the letter of the final sound in each word on the line under the picture.

1

w

2

_____

3

_____

4

_____

5

_____

6

_____

Name: _____ **Date:** _____

More Final Sounds to Name

Directions: Write the letter of the final sound in each word on the line under the picture.

❶ _____r_____

❷ _____

❸ _____

❹ _____

❺ _____

❻ _____

Name: _____ **Date:** _____

Ch or Sh?

....

Directions: Circle the beginning sound for each picture.

1 ch sh

2 ch sh

3 ch sh

4 ch sh

5 ch sh

6 ch sh

Name: _____ Date: _____

Tricky Beginning Sounds!

Directions: Circle the beginning sound for each picture.

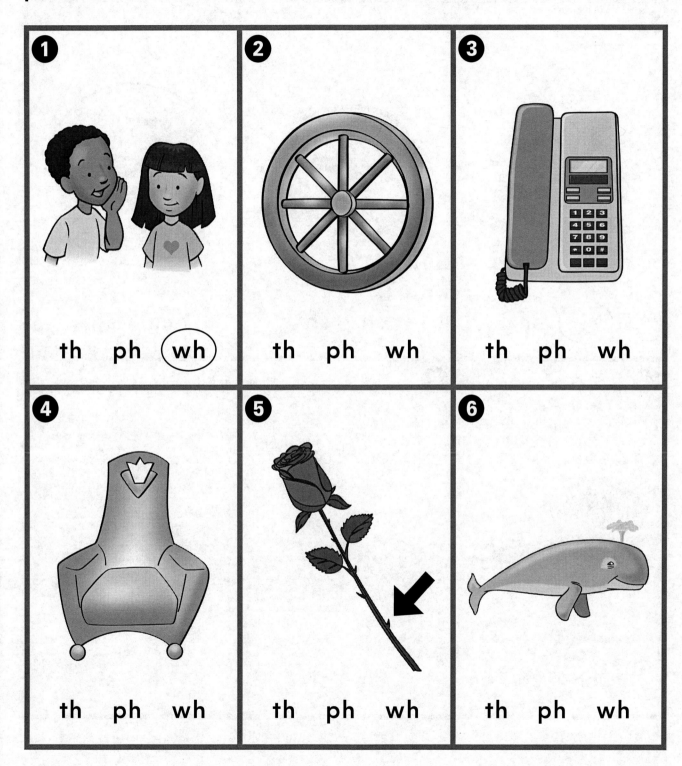

1

th ph (wh)

2

th ph wh

3

th ph wh

4

th ph wh

5

th ph wh

6

th ph wh

Name: _____ Date: _____

Tricky Ending Sounds!

Directions: Circle the ending sound for each picture.

1

(ch)   sh

2

ch   sh

3

ch   sh

4

ch   sh

5

ch   sh

6

ch   sh

#50884—Bright & Brainy: 1st Grade Practice

Name: _____ Date: _____

More Tricky Ending Sounds!

Directions: Circle the ending sound for each picture.

1

th (ck)

2

th   ck

3

th   ck

4

th   ck

5

th   ck

6

th   ck

Name: _____ **Date:** _____

What's That Word?

Directions: Draw a line from the picture to its name.

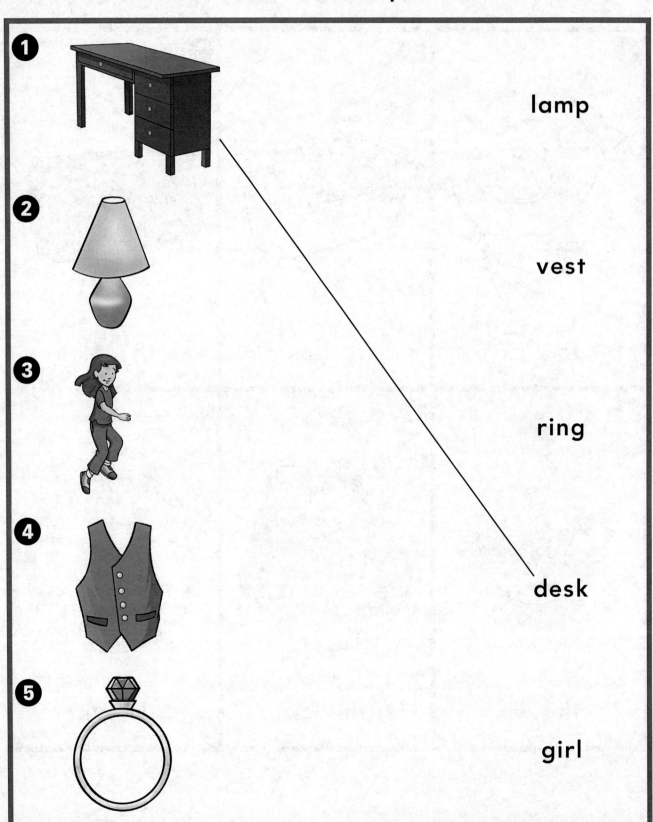

1   lamp

2   vest

3   ring

4   desk

5   girl

Name: _____ Date: _____

What Are These Words?

Directions: Draw a line from the picture to its name.

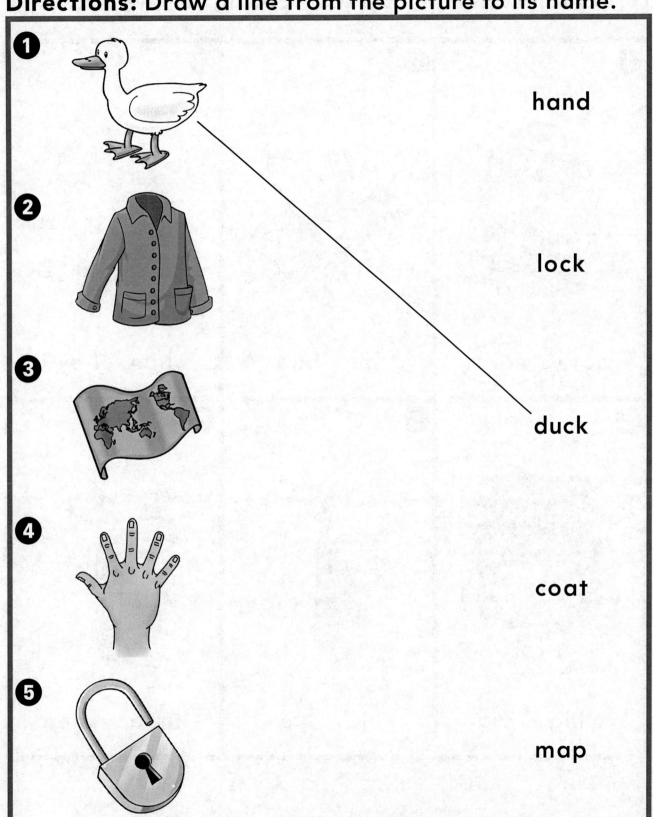

1. hand

2. lock

3. duck

4. coat

5. map

Name: _____ Date: _____

Spell It Right

Directions: Circle the correct spelling for the picture.

1 cote (coat)

2 be   bee

3 hae   hay

4 whig   wig

5 tie   tye

6 knea   knee

Name: _____ Date: _____

Spell More Right

Directions: Circle the correct spelling for the picture.

1 boat bote

2 wheel wheal

3 rain rane

4 gote goat

5 stool stule

6 hurn horn

Name: _____ **Date:** _____

How Many Parts?

Directions: Circle each vowel in the word. Count the syllables.

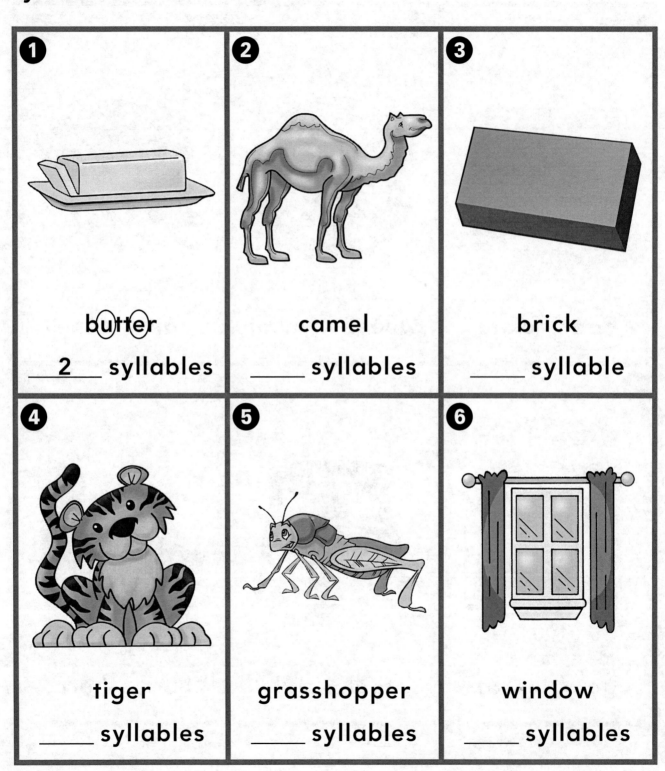

1 butter

___2___ syllables

2 camel

_____ syllables

3 brick

_____ syllable

4 tiger

_____ syllables

5 grasshopper

_____ syllables

6 window

_____ syllables

Name: _____ Date: _____

How Many Parts in These Words?

Directions: Circle each vowel in the word. Count the syllables.

❶ carrot

__2__ syllables

❷ banana

_____ syllables

❸ umbrella

_____ syllables

❹ horn

_____ syllable

❺ turkey

_____ syllables

❻ truck

_____ syllable

Name: _____ Date: _____

How Many Syllables?

Directions: Circle each vowel in the word. Count the syllables.

1 ch(e)r(ry)

__2__ syllables

2 wagon

____ syllables

3 zipper

____ syllables

4 backpack

____ syllables

5 kitty

____ syllables

6 spider

____ syllables

Name: _____ **Date:** _____

Read Longer Words

Directions: Draw a line from the word to its picture.

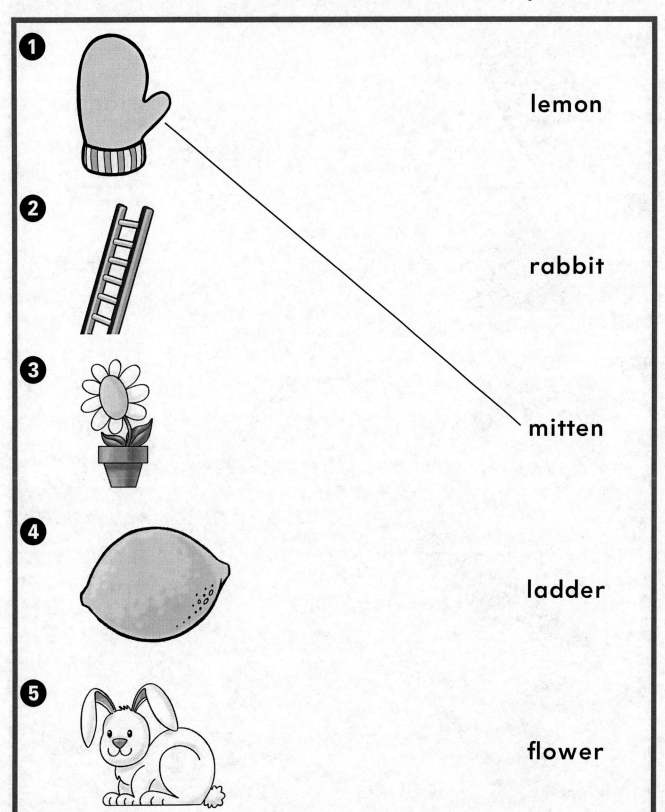

1. lemon

2. rabbit

3. mitten

4. ladder

5. flower

Name: _____ **Date:** _____

Read More Longer Words

Directions: Draw a line from the word to its picture.

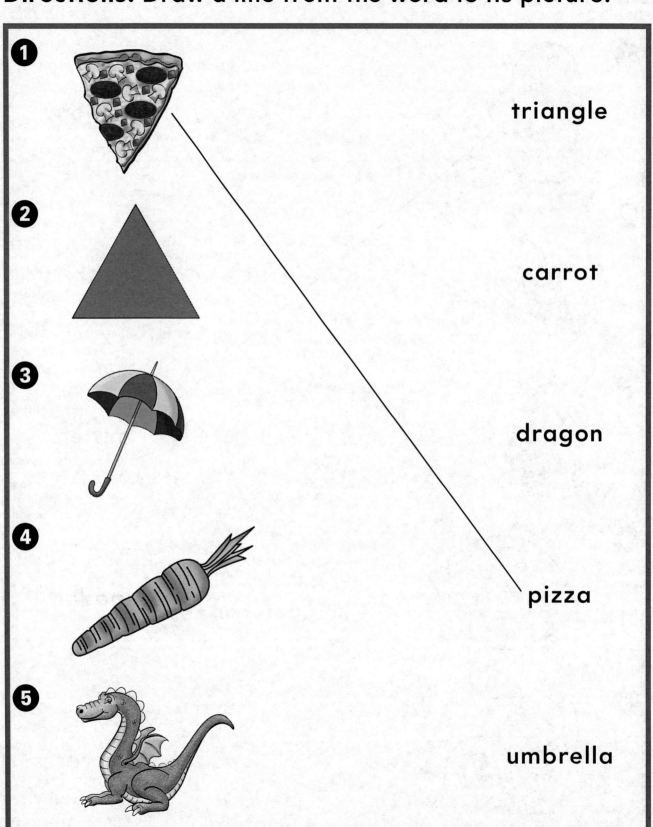

1. triangle

2. carrot

3. dragon

4. pizza

5. umbrella

#50884—*Bright & Brainy: 1st Grade Practice*

Name: _____ Date: _____

Learn About Endings

Directions: Add *–ly* to each word in the box. Then, write the word that best fits the meaning of the sentence.

loud_____

sad_____

safe __ly__

soft_____

quick_____

❶ He rides his bike ___safely___ .

❷ "Don't wake the baby," Mom said _____ .

❸ "My dog is lost," she said _____ .

❹ "We won the game!" Bob said _____ .

❺ He ran _____ down the hill.

Name: _____ Date: _____

Learn About More Endings

Directions: Add *-ing* to each word in the box. Then, write the word that best fits the meaning of the sentence.

> help_____
>
> look_____
>
> play_____
>
> sing_____
>
> thank _ing_

1 Mom is __thanking__ Dad.

2 Do you mind _____ pick up the toys?

3 Sam is _____ with his cat.

4 Pat is _____ to the baby.

5 Jane is _____ at the pets.

Name: _____ Date: _____

Read These Instant Words

Directions: Choose the right word from the box to finish the sentence. The words can be used more than once.

> This
>
> There
>
> These

1 _____ These _____ roses smell good.

2 _____ are lots of plants in the garden.

3 _____ tree is bigger than that tree.

4 _____ plants need water.

5 _____ will be rain soon.

Name: _____ Date: _____

Read More Instant Words

Directions: Choose the right word from the box to finish the sentence. The words can be used more than once.

We

What

Where

Who

1 _____Where_____ are we going?

2 _____ are going to the zoo.

3 _____ is going with us?

4 _____ are all going.

5 _____ time are we going?

Name: _____ Date: _____

Read Even More Instant Words

Directions: Choose the right word from the box to finish the sentence. The words can be used more than once.

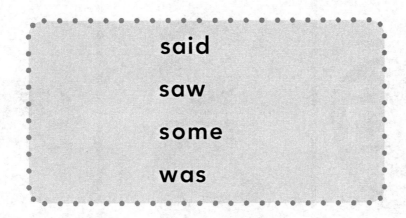

said

saw

some

was

1 Mom _____said_____ that we could swim.

2 I _____ toys in the pool.

3 Did you see _____ toys?

4 I _____ happy to be in the pool.

5 It _____ hot in the sun!

Name: _____ Date: _____

Print These Letters

Directions: Trace the letters.

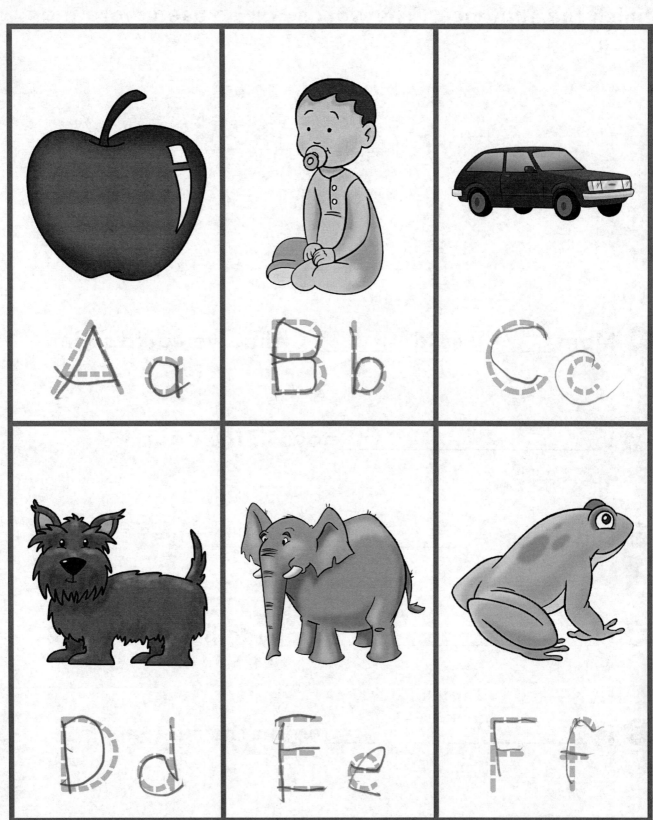

Name: _____ Date: _____

Print More Letters

Directions: Trace the letters.

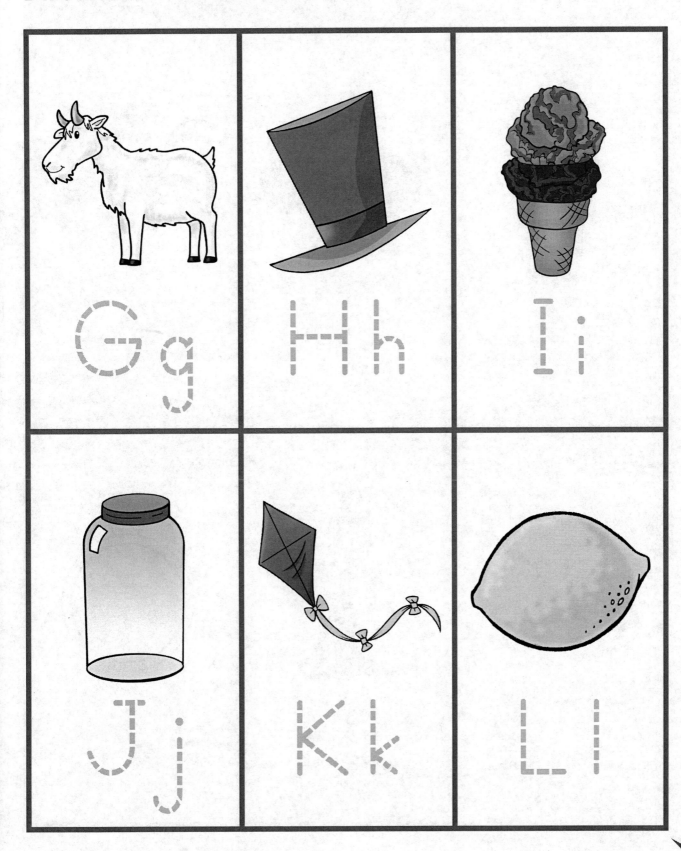

Name: _____ Date: _____

Print Even More Letters

Directions: Trace the letters.

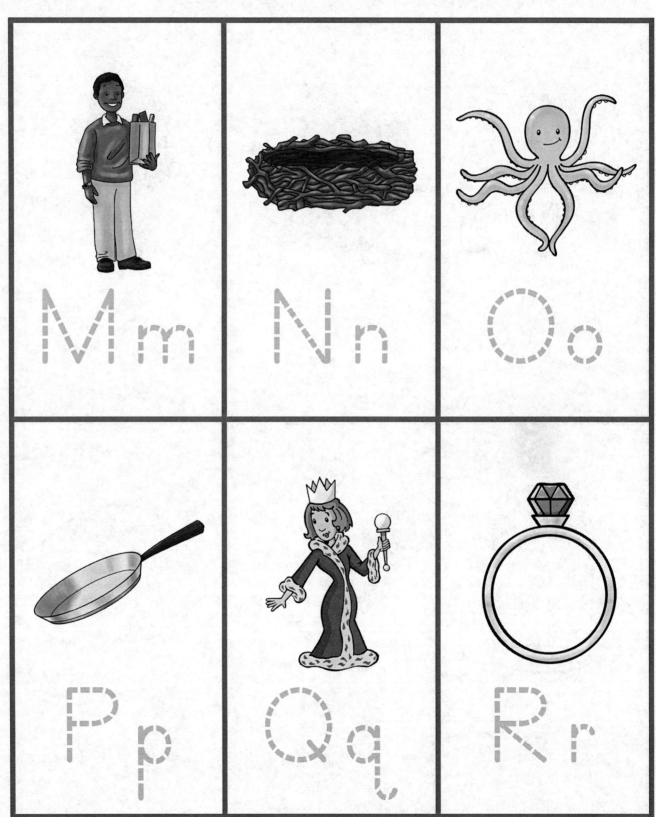

M m   N n   O o

P p   Q q   R r

Name: _____ Date: _____

Still More Letters

Directions: Trace the letters.

S s   T t   U u

V v   W w   X x

Y y   Z z

Name: _____ Date: _____

Name These Nouns

Directions: Draw a circle around the nouns that are asked for in each box.

People

(mother)	father	ask	child	hop	baby
aunt	go	girl	boy	big	

Places

run	(house)	on	farm	school
zoo	town	sit	wish	then

Things

if	(drum)	in	rope	boat
be	for	pan	lid	box

Ideas

(sadness)	if	happiness	where
surprise	when	anger	into

Name: _____ Date: _____

Naming More Nouns

A **common noun** names a general person, place, thing, or idea. A **proper noun** names something specific. It needs a capital letter.

Directions: Decide if each word is a common or proper noun. Shade the box in the correct column. Use the letters that remain to find out the answer to the riddle.

	Proper Nouns	Common Nouns
❶ Maria	b	a
❷ girl	m	n
❸ month	u	v
❹ California	r	s
❺ state	h	i
❻ Main Street Mall	q	r
❼ Mrs. Chase	b	o
❽ doctor	o	p
❾ lake	m	l

Question: What room is not part of a house or building?

$\underline{\quad a \quad}$ $\underline{\quad\quad}$ $\underline{\quad\quad}$ $\underline{\quad\quad}$ $\underline{\quad\quad}$ $\underline{\quad\quad}$ $\underline{\quad\quad}$ $\underline{\quad\quad}$ $\underline{\quad\quad}$
　　1　　2　　3　　4　　5　　6　　7　　8　　9

Name: _____ **Date:** _____

Show Ownership

....

A **possessive noun** shows ownership.

....

Directions: Add an apostrophe then an *s* to each word to show ownership.

1 It is the cat_'s_ dish.

2 It is Sam ____ job.

3 It is the boy ____ bat.

4 It is the girl ____ kitten.

5 It is Mom ____ pan.

Directions: Show possession.

1 a bone owned by a dog <u>the dog's bone</u>

2 a pig owned by a boy _____

3 a bike owned by Jose _____

4 a cap owned by Lia _____

5 a box owned by Kai _____

Name: _____ Date: _____

More Than One?

Directions: Write the number and noun for each picture below.

1

_____ 1 dog _____   _____ 2 dogs _____

2

_____   _____

3

_____   _____

4

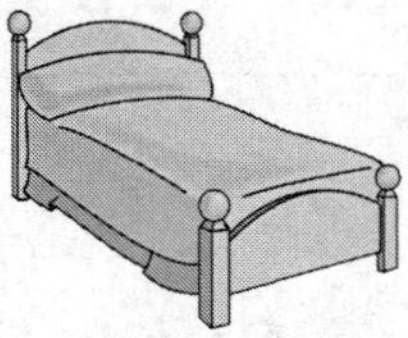

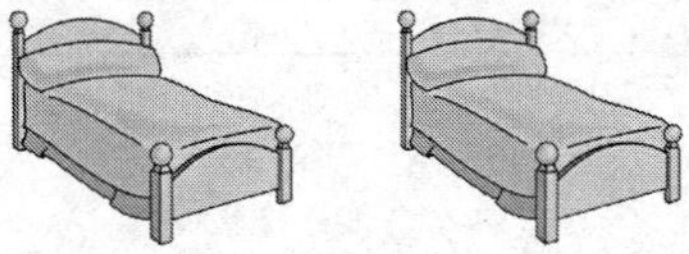

_____   _____

Name: _____ **Date:** _____

Which Is Plural?

Directions: Decide which underlined word should be plural. Rewrite the sentence with the correction.

1 Mom put three __jar__ of jam on the __table__ .

   Mom put three jars of jam on the table.

2 I need three <u>sheet</u> of <u>paper</u>.

   _____

   _____

   _____

3 My <u>room</u> has three <u>window</u>.

   _____

   _____

   _____

4 It is just three <u>day</u> until my <u>aunt</u> comes.

   _____

   _____

Name: _____ Date: _____

Plural or Possessive?

A **possessive noun** shows ownership.

Directions: Choose the right words to finish the sentence.

1 The __boys__ are playing baseball. One __boy's__ bat is made of wood.

boys   boy's

2 Two _____ ran up the tree. One

_____ tail got stuck.
cats   cat's

3 The _____ nest has three

_____ in it.
birds   bird's

4 The _____ pen does not have room for

more _____.
pigs   pig's

Name: _____ Date: _____

Pronoun Play

A **pronoun** can take the place of a noun in a sentence. Words like *he*, *him*, *her*, *she*, *I*, *we*, *they*, *it*, and *us* are pronouns.

Directions: Circle the pronouns in the paragraph.

The Circus

I was so happy when May first came. We were going to the circus! Mom got four tickets. She said I could ask a friend to come too. I asked Pat to come. When we got to the circus, the tent was huge. There were lots of clowns. They drove little cars. Then. a clown ran around with a bucket. Another clown chased him with a mop. He came right over to us. I thought he was going to dump water on us. But it was just bits of paper!

Name: _____ Date: _____

Pronouns at Work

Directions: Use a pronoun from the word bank in place of the underlined noun or nouns.

Word Bank

he	He	him	She	~~They~~

1 <u>Mom and Jose</u> went to the mall.

<u>They</u> went to the mall.

_____

2 <u>Mom</u> got a new coat.

_____

_____

_____

3 <u>Jose</u> wanted to look at games.

_____

_____

4 Jose saw his friend. He waved at <u>Sam</u>.

_____

_____

Name: _____ Date: _____

More Pronouns at Work

Directions: Use a pronoun from the word bank to finish each sentence.

Word Bank

All   ~~Anyone~~   Every   Everything   Nobody

1 _____Anyone_____ can come to our block party.

2 _____ game is fun.

3 _____ is free.

4 _____ will lose at the games.

5 _____ of my friends will come.

Name: _____ Date: _____

Take Action!

Verbs tell about action. Changing the ending on most verbs tells you about the time of action.

Directions: Write *past* or *present* in front of each sentence to tell the tense of the verb.

1 _____present_____ A man <u>fills</u> a pail with water.

2 _____ He <u>takes</u> the pail to the garden.

3 _____ A bee <u>buzzed</u> by.

4 _____ A man <u>stopped</u>.

Name: _____ **Date:** _____

Words in Action

....

Directions: Write *present* or *future* in front of each sentence to tell the tense of the verb.

1 _____ future _____ Jack <u>will ride</u> a pony tomorrow.

2 _____ Jack <u>hopes</u> it will be fun.

3 _____ Jack <u>will go</u> to the farm in the morning.

4 _____ Jack <u>packs</u> a bag with books and snacks for the ride.

Name: _____   Date: _____

More Words in Action

Directions: Write *past*, *present*, or *future* in front of each sentence to tell the tense of the verb.

1 _____past_____ Yesterday, I <u>baked</u> a cake.

2 _____ I <u>will</u> never <u>make</u> such a mess again.

3 _____ I <u>dropped</u> the eggs.

4 _____ My mom <u>reminds</u> me that it is fine to make mistakes.

Name: _____ Date: _____

Adjectives at Work

Adjectives are words that describe. They give more information about nouns.

Directions: Circle the adjectives in each sentence below. Then, underline the noun it describes. There may be more than one adjective in a sentence.

1 The (beautiful) <u>sailboat</u> is in the lake.

2 The big sail blows in the cool wind.

3 The hot sun feels good to the excited kids.

4 The fast boat speeds across the blue water.

5 The happy kids love the ride.

Name: _____ **Date:** _____

More Adjectives at Work

Directions: Choose an adjective from the Word Bank to describe each picture.

Word Bank

~~fluffy~~ huge tall happy

1 _fluffy_ cloud

2 _____ girl

3 _____ elephant

4 _____ hat

Name: _____ **Date:** _____

Useful Adjectives

Directions: Use adjectives from the box to finish the story.

How many?	What kind?
some	bad
one	purple
	striped

Last week I had a _____

day. I had _____ hair! I

had to do something! So I filled the sink with

_____ soap. Then it got worse.

Now I had _____ hair. I was just

having _____ bad day!

Name: _____ Date: _____

Put It Together

Conjunctions join words or sentences together.

Directions: Fill in each blank with a conjunction from in the Word Bank.

Word Bank

and   or

1 Do you have a big _____or_____ little dog?

2 I like both big _____ little dogs.

3 My little dog is black, _____ my big dog is white.

4 My friend has cats _____ fish.

Name: _____ **Date:** _____

Combining Sentences

··

> **Conjunctions** can help combine two sentences.

Directions: Combine the sentences below using the conjunction *and* or *or*.

❶ Mom got us new clothes. Dad got us new clothes.

Mom and Dad got us new clothes.
_____

❷ I had carrots for dinner. I had chicken for dinner.

_____

_____

❸ I don't have a pencil. I don't have a pen.

_____

_____

❹ Could I borrow your pencil? Could I borrow your pen?

_____

_____

Name: _____ Date: _____

More Words to Combine

Conjunctions can join words or sentences together.

Directions: Use the conjunctions in the Word Bank to fill in the blanks.

Word Bank

and   because   but   or   so

1 The game ended <u>because</u> of the rain.

2 I like art _____ math.

3 Mom said I could play, _____ I had to do my homework first.

4 I said it didn't matter. Either

pizza _____ chicken

would be fine.

Name: _____ **Date:** _____

Useful Little Words

....

Articles tell you that a noun is coming next. Three important articles are the words *a*, *an*, and *the*.

Directions: Circle the article. Underline the noun that comes after it.

1 Dad fixed (the) <u>dinner</u>.

2 He made soup in a pot.

3 He baked the bread.

4 He peeled an orange for each salad.

5 I put the plates away.

Name: _____ Date: _____

This and That

> *This* and *that* are **adjectives**. They tell you that a noun is coming next.

Directions: Circle the article. Underline the noun.

1 I read (that) <u>book</u>.

2 I read this book, too.

3 Did you like that story?

4 The ending in this book was best.

5 Don't read that book at night.

Name: _____ **Date:** _____

These and Those

These and *those* are **adjectives.** They tell you that a noun is coming next.

Directions: Circle the article. Underline the noun.

1 I like (these) clothes.

2 They are warmer than those clothes.

3 Those pants are good for sledding.

4 These nights are so cold.

5 Don't forget those mittens.

Name: _____ **Date:** _____

Preposition Play

Words that tell you about where something is are called **prepositions**.

Directions: Choose a word from the Word Bank to show where each ball is.

Word Bank

~~above~~   behind   inside   under

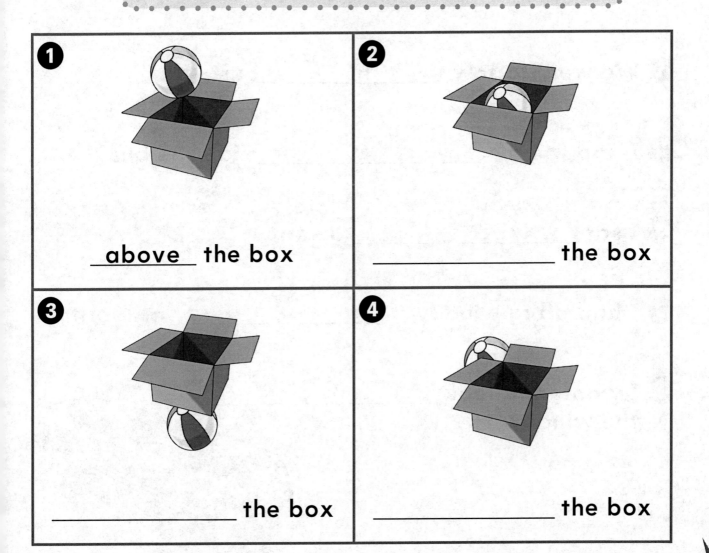

1 ___above___ the box

2 _____ the box

3 _____ the box

4 _____ the box

Name: _____ **Date:** _____

More Preposition Play

Words that tell you about where something is are called **prepositions**.

Directions: Choose a preposition from the Word Bank to complete each sentence.

Word Bank

on   in   to   beside   out

❶ We went to town ____in____ a bus.

❷ I had to pay _____ ride the bus.

❸ I sat _____ a seat.

❹ I had a big window _____ my seat.

❺ I wanted to look _____ the window.

Name: _____ Date: _____

When, Where, Which Way?

Directions: Circle the prepositions. Write whether the preposition tells when, where, or which way.

1 I was playing (in) my room.

_____ where _____

2 She went down the slide.

_____

3 I put the game on the shelf.

_____

4 I sat at my desk and worked hard.

_____

5 After an hour, my homework was done.

_____

Name: _____ Date: _____

Sentence Detective

A **sentence** has a complete thought.

Directions: Write *yes* by the complete sentences. Write *no* by the phrases.

_____ **1** in the dog house

_____ **2** Spot has some bones.

_____ **3** a hole under the big tree

_____ **4** When you are

_____ **5** It's great!

Name: _____ Date: _____

Ask a Question, Okay?

Directions: Read each answer. Then, write the question.

1 Question: Do you like apples? _____

Answer: Yes, I like apples.

2 Question: _____

_____

_____

Answer: My bedroom is blue.

3 Question: _____

_____

_____

Answer: I have one dog.

4 Question: _____

_____

_____

Answer: I rode my bike to school.

Name: _____ **Date:** _____

Which Kind of Sentence?

An **imperative sentence** gives a command.
A **declarative sentence** makes a statement.

Directions: Write the letter *I* by the imperative sentences. Write the letter *D* by the declarative sentences.

1 ____I____ Come here now!

2 _____ It's getting late.

3 _____ Get all those toys picked up now!

4 _____ This is the best day.

5 _____ I like playing here.

Name: _____ Date: _____

Put These Together

A **compound sentence** needs complete thoughts.

Directions: Join the sentence to make a compound sentence.

1 I like playing soccer. I like watching soccer.
<u>I like playing soccer, and I like watching soccer.</u>

2 I went to bed. I dreamed all night.

_____

_____

_____

3 We packed up the car. We left quickly.

_____

_____

_____

4 Do you like dogs? Do you like cats?

_____

_____

_____

Name: _____ **Date:** _____

Find the Right Noun

Names of people are **proper nouns.** They start with a capital letter.

Directions: Choose the correct noun from each pair.

1 ____Ben____ went to the park with his ___brother___.
Ben ben   Brother brother

2 _____ told him to wear a _____.
Mom mom   Hat hat

3 Please tell _____ that we are going.
Dad dad

4 I will take my _____, too.
Dog dog

5 I love taking _____ to the park.
Duke duke

Name: _____ Date: _____

Make Them Proper!

The names of days and months are **proper nouns**. They start with a capital letter.

Directions: Circle the words that should begin with a capital letter. *Hint:* One sentence does not have any proper nouns.

1 I like to watch the football games on (january) first!

2 The first day of the year came on a monday.

3 My birthday is on february 29th.

4 My birthday comes once every four years.

5 Last year, my birthday came on a friday.

Name: _____ Date: _____

Punctuation Station

Directions: Write a period, question mark, or exclamation point at the end of each sentence.

1 I love going to the zoo__!__

2 We always take a snack along _____

3 What would you bring to eat _____

4 We go see the elephants first _____

5 They are huge _____

Name: _____ Date: _____

More at the Punctuation Station

Directions: Write a punctuation mark at the end of each sentence.

Frogs

Frogs are fun to learn about ____ One

frog is called a glass frog ____ You can

see through its skin ____ Have you heard

of the water holding frog ____ It takes

in water through its skin ____ It uses the

water during dry times ____ One kind of

frog looks just like a turtle ____ What do

you think it is called ____ Yes, it's called a

turtle frog ____ I think frogs are fun ____

Do you ____

Name: _____ Date: _____

Punctuate and Capitalize

Directions: Circle the words that need capital letters. Write a punctuation mark at the end of each sentence.

Jumbo

have you heard of Jumbo _____ He was a

huge elephant _____ he was about 12 feet

tall _____ For many years, he was at the

london Zoo _____ That is where he got the

name of jumbo _____ for years he was in

a circus _____ Sadly, Jumbo was hit by a

train _____ He was 24 years old _____

Name: _____ Date: _____

Commas in Lists

Use a **comma** between three or more words in a list.

Directions: Add the missing commas to the sentences below.

1 I packed our hats, gloves, and socks.

2 Dad put our skis poles and helmets in the van.

3 We put in our skates scarves and goggles, too.

4 My mom brought out boots sleds and snow shoes.

5 We looked at the van. Where would we put snacks drinks and Fido?

Name: _____ **Date:** _____

Commas in Sentences

Directions: Add commas to the combined sentences.
Hint: Some are not combined sentences.

1 Did you know that whales talk? Some whales click, and some whales sing.

2 Some whales seem to bark but some seem to whistle.

3 Sometimes it seems like the whales talk to each other.

4 One whale makes some clicks and then it stops.

5 Another whale makes clicks and it stops, too.

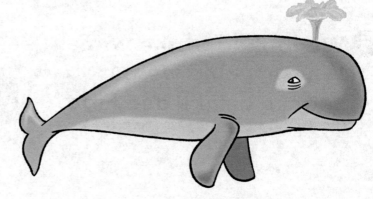

Name: _____ Date: _____

Commas and More

Directions: Add commas to the sentences with dates. Add an end punctuation mark where it is needed.

1 Mom was born on June 20, 1980 ___.___

2 My sister was born on June 20 2011 _____

3 They were born exactly 31 years apart _____ Isn't that funny _____

4 My dad was born on July 4 1980 _____

5 Boom _____ Dad says the fireworks are all for him _____

Name: _____ Date: _____

Spelling Patterns

Directions: Spell the word for each picture.

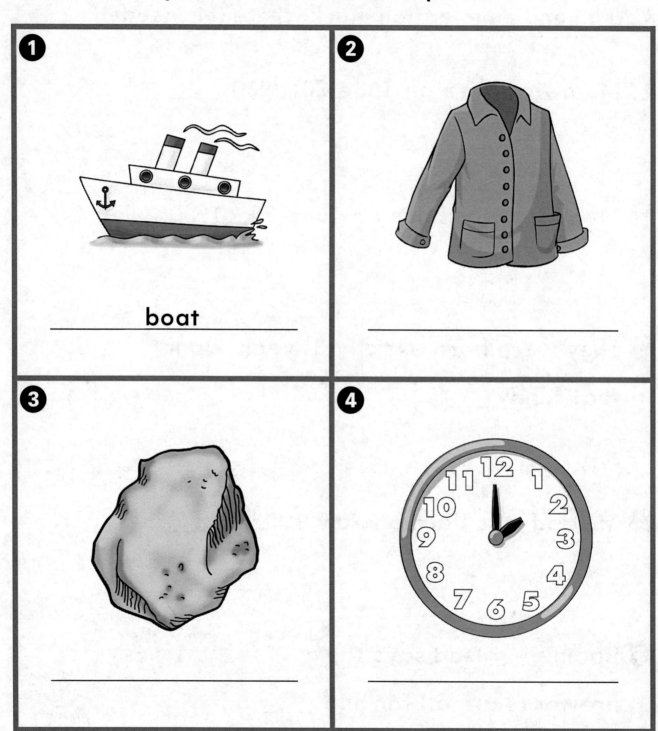

❶

boat

❷

_____

❸

_____

❹

_____

Name: _____ **Date:** _____

More Spelling Patterns

Directions: Spell the word for each picture.

1 hair

2

3

4

Name: _____ **Date:** _____

Text Fun

Directions: Read the paragraph. Then, answer the questions.

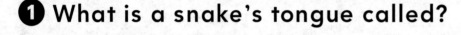

Have you ever seen a snake's tongue? It is long, and it's split down the middle. It is called a forked tongue. A snake's tongue flicks in and out as it moves. The tongue helps it smell. That helps the snake know what is around it.

❶ What is a snake's tongue called?

A forked tongue.

❷ Is a snake's tongue short or long?

long.

❸ How does the tongue help the snake?

It helps it smell.

❹ What would be a good title for this text?

snakes.

Name: _____ Date: _____

More Text Fun

Directions: Read the paragraph. Then, answer the questions.

Have you ever seen a cat wash its face? It is keeping its whiskers clean. Those stiff hairs are useful. A cat can use them to tell how to get around. They are about as wide as the cat's head. They help tell how big an opening is. Cats can still get stuck. But, they would get stuck more without whiskers!

1 Why does a cat wash its face?

_____

2 What are whiskers?

_____

3 How big are the whiskers?

_____

4 What would be a good title for this text?

_____

Name: _____ Date: _____

Another Text

Directions: Read the paragraph. Then, answer the questions.

You can tell a lot about a dog by its tail. A stiff tail means you should be careful. The dog may be upset. Is the tail wagging slowly? That dog may be upset, too. Is the dog wagging its whole back end? Then it may be happy. No matter what its tail seems to say, ask the owner if you can meet the dog.

❶ What might a stiff tail mean?

_____

❷ What might a happy dog do?

_____

❸ What should you do when you want to meet a dog?

_____

❹ What would be a good title for this text?

_____

Name: _____ Date: _____

Read This Text

Directions: Read the paragraph. Then, answer the questions.

There is a good reason why stink bugs got their name. When they are crushed, they stink! Stink bugs are less than an inch long. They have six legs. They have wings. They eat leaves, fruits, and flowers. They can hurt a lot of crops. If you ever kill a stink bug, you will know it. Phew!

1 How big are stink bugs?

_____

2 How many legs do they have?

_____

3 What do they like to eat?

_____

4 What would be a good title for this text?

_____

_____

Name: _____ **Date:** _____

A Squirrel Story

Directions: Read the paragraph. Then, answer the questions.

About Squirrels

A gray squirrel eats about two pounds of food each week. It eats roots and fruit. Gray squirrels seem to plan for winter. A squirrel buries more than 1,000 nuts. Later, they use their sense of smell to find them. If they forget a nut, it might grow into a tree!

❶ How much food does a squirrel eat each week?

a. 1,000 nuts

b. two pounds

c. roots

❷ How does a squirrel plan for winter?

a. It buries nuts.

b. It eats a lot of nuts.

c. It eats roots and fruit.

❸ How do gray squirrels find their nuts?

a. They leave them in one big pile.

b. They dig in lots of places.

c. They use their sense of smell.

❹ What is the main idea of this text?

a. A nut can grow into a tree.

b. Gray squirrels bury nuts to eat in winter.

c. Gray squirrels have a strong sense of smell.

Name: _____ Date: _____

A Hedgehog Story

Directions: Read the paragraph. Then, answer the questions.

Hedgehogs

A hedgehog is a small animal. It weighs around one pound. It has three ways to stay safe. It has spines on its back. It can roll into a ball, and the spines stick out. A hedgehog can also run fast. It has one more way to stay safe. It can roll into a ball and just roll away!

1 What does a hedgehog have on its back?

a. fur

b. spines

c. skin

2 How big is a hedgehog?

a. about a pound

b. about as big as a cat

c. about two pounds

3 What can a hedgehog do to stay safe?

a. roll into a ball and roll away

b. shoot spines

c. scratch and bite

4 What is the main idea of the text?

a. Hedgehogs live in many places.

b. Hedgehogs know how to get away from danger.

c. Hedgehogs make funny pets.

Name: _____ Date: _____

Snurfers

Directions: Read the paragraph. Then, answer the questions.

New Invention

Have you heard of a Snurfer? One day a girl stood on her sled to go down a hill. Her dad saw her. He tied up two skis to make one board. He put a rope at one end. The girl could stand and glide down the hills. Her mom called it a Snurfer. Since then, the Snurfer has changed. Lots of people ride it. But, now it is called a snowboard.

❶ What did the dad use to make a Snurfer?

    a. a ski and a rope

    b. 2 skis and a rope

    c. a sled and a rope

❷ Who did he make it for?

    a. his son

    b. his wife

    c. his daughter

❸ Who thought of the name Snurfer?

    a. the mom

    b. the dad

    c. a girl

❹ What is the main idea of the text?

    a. how the snowboard began

    b. how the sled changed

    c. a family had fun

#50884—*Bright & Brainy: 1st Grade Practice*

Name: _____ Date: _____

Rescue Dogs

Directions: Read the paragraph. Then, answer the questions.

Smart Dogs

How can a dog find someone buried under snow? It uses its nose. A dog has a great sense of smell. It is about 50 times stronger than yours. A good rescue dog should have a long nose. The dog must be smart. It has to be strong. It may need to track through deep snow. The dog is trained for weeks. It works very hard. It must be ready when someone needs help.

1 What does a rescue dog use to find a person?

  a. its paws

  b. its ears

  c. its nose

2 Why do you think rescue dogs are trained for weeks?

  a. They like to play.

  b. They may need to rescue someone.

  c. They are smart.

3 How are dogs different from you?

  a. They have a better sense of smell.

  b. They see better.

  c. They like to work.

4 What is the main idea of this text?

  a. Rescue dogs are trained to use their sense of smell.

  b. Rescue dogs like to track and dig in the snow.

  c. A smart dog can be a rescue dog.

Name: _____ **Date:** _____

Using a Table of Contents

Directions: Read the table of contents. Then, answer the questions.

Table of Contents

❶ **What is the book about?**

  a. fish
  b. dolphins
  c. playing in the sea

❷ **What page tells about what dolphins eat?**

  a. page 10
  b. page 12
  c. page 14

Name: _____ Date: _____

More about Using a Table of Contents

Directions: Read the table of contents. Then, answer the questions.

Table of Contents

1 You want to find out how snakes move. What page should you go to?

  a. page 8
  b. page 18
  c. page 22

2 You want to find out how to feed a snake. What page should you go to?

  a. page 6
  b. page 12
  c. page 18

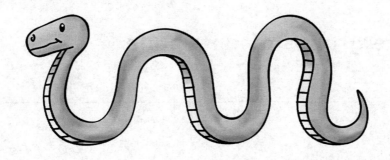

Name: _____ Date: _____

Picture Reading

Directions: Read the text. Look at the picture. Then, answer the questions.

Meet an Ant!

Ants can be found almost everywhere. They live in groups called colonies. They share the work to keep the colony going. Some ants can kill plants. They are called pests. But, some ants eat other insects. Those ants are helpful. Did you know that some people like to eat ants? There is a lot to learn about ants!

head

thorax

abdomen

❶ List the three main parts to an ant's body.

_____

_____

_____

❷ How many legs does an ant have? _____

❸ What are groups of ants called?

_____

Name: _____ Date: _____

More Picture Reading

Directions: Read the text. Look at the picture. Then, answer the questions.

Meet an African Elephant

Elephants in Africa are very big. The males may be more than 10 feet tall. They may weigh more than 10,000 pounds. The female elephants are smaller. Elephants have flat feet and big toenails. They can pick up things with their trunks. They use their tusks to dig and fight.

tusks
ears
tail
trunk
feet
toenails

❶ How many tusks does an elephant have? _____

❷ Is the male or female elephant bigger?

_____

❸ Name two things an elephant can do with its tusks.

_____

_____

Name: _____ Date: _____

Another Text and Picture

Directions: Read the text. Look at the picture. Then, answer the questions.

Meet a Robin

The robin is a songbird. You may hear it sing. Robins start their families in the spring. The male robin helps build the nest. The female lays three to five eggs. The babies are born in about two weeks. Both the male and female robin feed and take care of the baby robins. The babies love to eat worms. Soon, the baby robins can fly. But, they may still follow their parents. They want more worms from them!

head
wing
beak
feet

❶ How many eggs does a female bird lay?

_____

❷ Why is a robin called a songbird?

_____

_____

❸ When do robins start their families? _____

_____

_____

Name: _____ Date: _____

One More Text and Picture

Directions: Read the text. Look at the picture. Then, answer the questions.

The Tree You Don't See

Take a look at a tree. Did you know a big part of it is under the ground? A tree may be 20 feet high. Its roots might be just as deep! Roots have important jobs. They take water from the ground up to the tree. They also take food, called nutrients. They also keep the tree from falling over in the wind. Next time you look up at a tree, look down too!

leaves

branches

trunk

soil

roots

❶ Name three parts of the tree that are above the ground.

_____

_____

_____

❷ Name two jobs that the roots do.

_____

_____

Name: _____ Date: _____

Mice Are Nice

Directions: Read the text. Look at the picture. Then, answer the questions.

About Mice

Mice make great pets. They are cute. They are smart. They are easy to tame. People think they are dirty. But, they like to stay clean. Just watch one for a while. You will see it wash itself. Mice are quiet. They are easy to feed. There is just one thing I do not like about mice. They have short lives. If you think that you would like a mouse, go to a pet store. You want to make sure your pet is healthy and safe.

❶ What are three good things about pet mice?

_____

_____

❷ What does the author not like about mice?

_____

❸ Do you agree with the author that mice make great pets? Why or why not?

_____

_____

_____

Name: _____ Date: _____

The Best Invention

Directions: Read the text. Look at the picture.
Then, answer the questions.

Bikes!

The bicycle is the best invention. Bikes come in all sizes. There are bikes made for all ages. Babies can even ride in a trailer pulled by a bike. You can pedal with your feet. You can pedal with your hands with special bikes. Some people may think cars are a better invention. But, bikes do not need gas. And, you get exercise too! Bikes are the best!

❶ What are three good things about bikes?

_____

_____

❷ Why does the author think bikes are better than cars?

_____

_____

❸ Do you agree with the author that bikes are the best invention? Why or why not?

_____

_____

Name: _____ Date: _____

What's That About?

Directions: Circle the picture that goes with the sentence.

1 I can brush my hair.		
2 Here comes a ball. Duck!		
3 I like to bowl.		
4 Pam fans her face.		
5 Block the ball!		

Name: _____ Date: _____

What's That Mean?

Directions: Circle the picture that goes with the sentence.

1 Watch me skate.	 
2 Jon likes to fish.	 
3 Tie your shoes.	 
4 I saw the boy pet the dog.	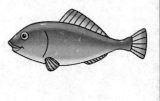 
5 Ring the bell!	 

Name: _____ Date: _____

Choose the Picture

Directions: Circle the picture that goes with the sentence.

1 He likes to train dogs.	 
2 Water the plant.	 
3 Watch the road!	 
4 Put the pig in the pen.	 
5 The boys play ball.	 

Name: _____ Date: _____

Prefix Match

A **prefix** is a word part added to the beginning of a word. It changes the meaning.

The prefix *un-* and *dis-*means *not.*

Directions: Draw a line to match the word with its meaning.

1 distrust   not in place

2 displace   not curled

3 uncurl   not packed

4 unclear   not trusted

5 unpack   not clear

Name: _____ Date: _____

More Prefix Match

A **prefix** is a word part added to the beginning of a word. It changes the meaning.

The prefix *over-* can mean *too much* and *above*.

The prefix *under-* can mean *less than* and *below*.

Directions: Draw a line to match the word with its meaning.

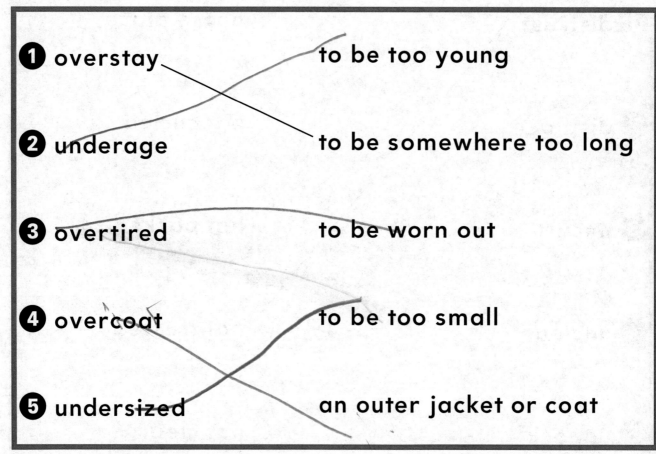

1 overstay   to be too young

2 underage   to be somewhere too long

3 overtired   to be worn out

4 overcoat   to be too small

5 undersized   an outer jacket or coat

Name: _____ Date: _____

Suffix Choices

....

A **suffix** is a word part added to the end of a word. It changes the meaning.

The suffixes *-er* and *-est* can mean more. Add *-er* when comparing two things.

Directions: Choose the correct word.

1 This is the _____biggest_____ rock in the pile.

big   bigger   (biggest)

2 A turtle is _____ than a rabbit.

slow   slower   slowest

3 Dad is taller than Mom. Uncle Tom is

the _____ in our family.

tall   taller   tallest

4 It is the _____ day of the year.

cold   colder   coldest

Name: _____ Date: _____

Work with Suffixes

Directions: Finish the sentences by changing the given word.

❶ That is the <u>heaviest</u> book on the shelf.

heavy

❷ That clown is _____ than the one in the car.

funny

❸ My baby sister can be so _____.

silly

❹ The movie was _____ than the other one.

scary

Name: _____ Date: _____

Suffix Match

A **suffix** is a word part added to the ending of a word. It changes the meaning.

The suffix *-ful* means *full of.*

The suffix *-less* means *without.*

Directions: Draw a line to match the word with its meaning.

1 fearful   to have no place to live

2 endless   to hurt a lot

3 helpful   to be scared

4 painful   something that seems to never stop

5 homeless   to help out

Name: _____ Date: _____

Good Sports!

....

Directions: Write the words in the right category.

Word Bank

baseball	catcher	surfboard	skis
basketball	football	surfer	snowboard
boxer	ice skates	skater	soccer ball
bowler	runner	skier	swimmer

Things in sports	People in sports

Name: _____ Date: _____

Good Work!

Directions: Write the words in the right category.

Word Bank

computer	farmer	painter	ruler
dancer	hammer	paper	saw
desk	mop	pilot	teacher
doctor	nurse	rake	writer

Tools or things used at work	Workers

Name: _____ Date: _____

Buildings and Places

Directions: Write the words in the right category.

Word Bank

bus station	country	house	school
café	factory	library	seaport
church	field	neighborhood	town
city	fire station	park	village

Buildings	Places

Name: _____ Date: _____

Taking Action or Having Feelings?

Directions: Write the words in the right category.

Word Bank

find	joy	sorrow	thrilled
happiness	clap	start	afraid
give	play	take	scared
help	share	thankful	worried

Emotions or feelings	Action

Name: _____ Date: _____

What Does It Mean?

Directions: Find a word from each box that helps describe it. Some words can be used more than once.

Word Bank		
noun	**adjective**	
animal	big	furry
insect	long	little
person	small	tiny
vehicle	wild	

	noun	**adjective**
1 dog	animal	furry
2 bee		
3 bear		
4 baby		
5 airplane		

Name: _____ Date: _____

Tell All About It!

Directions: Find a word from each box that helps describe it. Some words can be used more than once.

Word Bank

noun	adjective	
food	big	red
person	female	tall
vehicle	round	white
plant	green	

	noun	**adjective**
❶ apple	food	red
❷ egg		
❸ bike		
❹ mother		
❺ tree		

Name: _____ Date: _____

Make the Connection!

Directions: Match the words from the box onto the lines. Some words can be used more than once.

Word Bank

bedroom	park
garage	street
home	yard
library	

1 quiet _____bedroom, library, home_____

2 parade _____

3 party _____

4 picnic _____

5 noise _____

Name: _____ Date: _____

Where Might It Be?

Directions: Match the words from the box onto the lines. Some words can be used more than once.

Word Bank

mountains	street
park	yard
river	zoo
store	

1 wild animals   <u>zoo, mountains, river</u>

2 fun   _____

3 slide   _____

4 trees   _____

5 friends   _____

Name: _____ Date: _____

Meaning Match!

Directions: Find a similar meaning for each word.

Word Bank

amaze	shout
begin	speak
~~question~~	

1 ask _____question_____

2 surprise _____

3 start _____

4 yell _____

5 talk _____

Name: _____ Date: _____

Noun Match!

Directions: Find a similar meaning for each word.

Word Bank

~~auto~~   pair

present   trash

work

1 car _____ auto _____

2 gift _____

3 job _____

4 junk _____

5 couple _____

Name: _____ Date: _____

Another Adjective!

Directions: Find a similar meaning for each word.

Word Bank

~~aged~~	flat
glad	tiny
grand	

1 old _____aged_____

2 level _____

3 large _____

4 little _____

5 happy _____

Name: _____ Date: _____

Meaning Magic!

Directions: Find a similar meaning for each word.

> ## Word Bank
>
> all   bother
>
> fat   end
>
> near

1 close   near _____

2 plump   _____

3 every   _____

4 pester   _____

5 finish   _____

Name: _____ Date: _____

The Frogs Who Wanted a King

Directions: Read the story below. Then, answer the questions.

Wishing for a King

Four frogs lived in a pond. One was big and three were little. All day long, they jumped about. They swam. They had fun. One day, the big frog said he thought it would be more fun to have a king. The other frogs agreed. They all wished for a king. The next day, a branch fell off a tree. The frogs thought it must be their king. They talked to it. They jumped on it. They pushed at it. It did not move. It did not talk. The small frogs gave up. They went back to jumping and splashing. The big frog sat on the log. He thought, "I know. I think we need a queen!"

Name: _____ Date: _____

The Frogs Who Wanted a King (cont.)

1 What do the frogs do before the king comes?

   a. They croaked and dived.

   (b.) They swam and jumped.

   c. They caught flies.

2 Why does the big frog want a king?

   a. The other frogs are small.

   b. The other frogs don't do what he wants.

   (c.) He thinks it would be even more fun.

3 What do the frogs do to the branch?

   (a.) They talk to it.

   b. They sleep on it.

   c. They swim by it.

4 Why do the small frogs give up on the king?

   a. They are tired.

   b. They are mad at the big frog.

   (c.) It does not move or say anything.

Name: _____ Date: _____

The Fox, the Rooster, and the Dog

Directions: Read the story. Then, answer the questions.

Fast Fox

A fox was hungry. He saw a hen high up on a henhouse. He thought he would trick the hen.

"Hello, Friend!" said the fox. "I have good news!"

"I don't think you'd have news for me," said the hen.

The fox said, "The king has said we must all be friends. Come on down!"

"What?" said the hen. "That is good news. Here comes the dog. He will be happy to hear your news."

"Oh...never mind," said the fox. "I would tell him. But he might not believe me."

The fox ran off. And that is how the hen lived to tell her story.

Name: _____ Date: _____

The Fox, the Rooster, and the Dog *(cont.)*

❶ Why does the fox try to trick the hen?

   a. He wants to be her friend.

   b. He wants to meet the dog.

   c. He wants to eat her.

❷ What does the hen tell the fox?

   a. He should tell the dog about being friends.

   b. She will come down.

   c. She doesn't believe him.

❸ Why does the fox run off?

   a. The dog is probably big and mean.

   b. The dog will want to play with the fox.

   c. The dog will eat the hen.

❹ What happens to the hen?

   a. She has her dinner.

   b. She lives to tell her story.

   c. She goes in the henhouse.

❺ What lesson do you think the fox learns?

_____

_____

_____

Name: _____ Date: _____

The Wind or the Sun?

Directions: Read the story. Then, answer the questions.

Who's Stronger?

The wind and the sun were good friends. But one day, they began to fight.

"I know you are strong," said the sun. "But I am stronger."

"I don't think so," said the wind. "You can make it hot. But, I can blow things around."

They fought and fought. One day they saw a man walking along.

"I know what to do," said the sun. "Let's see who can make him take his coat off."

"That's easy," said the wind. "I'll blow his coat off."

The sun hid behind a cloud. The wind blew and blew. The man just pulled his coat tighter.

"Give up!" said the sun. "Now it's my turn. Watch this."

The wind stopped blowing. The sun came out from behind the cloud. The man looked up at the sun.

"Where did the wind go? It is so warm. I can take my coat off."

And he did.

Name: _____ Date: _____

The Wind or the Sun? *(cont.)*

1 What do the sun and wind fight about?

   a. who is bigger

   b. who is stronger

   c. who is faster

2 What does the sun do while the wind blows?

   a. hide behind the wind

   b. hide behind the mountain

   c. hide behind a cloud

3 What does the man do when the wind blows?

   a. pull his coat tighter

   b. pull off his coat

   c. pull on his hat

4 Why does the man take off his coat?

   a. The wind has stopped.

   b. It gets hot.

   c. The rain has stopped.

5 Do you think the sun is stronger or smarter than the wind? Why?

_____

_____

_____

Name: _____ Date: _____

The Grasshopper and the Ant

Directions: Read the story. Then, answer the questions.

Prepare for Winter

One summer day, a grasshopper hopped and sang. The ant took an ear of corn to its nest.

"Why are you working so hard?" said the grasshopper. "You should play with me!"

"Winter is coming," said the ant. "You should save some food, too."

"I'm not worried," said the grasshopper. "There is plenty of time. I want to play."

The ant worked. The grasshopper played. Soon summer was over. Winter came. The grasshopper had no food. He went to the ant for help.

"I am dying of hunger," the grasshopper said to the ant. "Can you help me?"

"I am sorry," said the ant. "If I help you, my family will go hungry."

The grasshopper left. He had learned his lesson.

Name: _____ Date: _____

The Grasshopper and the Ant (cont.)

❶ Why does the ant work hard?

   a. He wants food for the winter.

   b. He likes working.

   c. He is strong.

❷ Why doesn't the grasshopper save food?

   a. He can't find any.

   b. He is mad at the ant.

   c. He isn't worried about winter.

❸ Why does the grasshopper go to see the ant that winter?

   a. He wants to sing and play.

   b. He wants some food.

   c. He wants to say he is sorry.

❹ Why doesn't the ant help him?

   a. He is hungry.

   b. He needs to save his food.

   c. He needs to save his family.

❺ What lesson does the grasshopper learn?

_____

_____

_____

Name: _____ **Date:** _____

Book Log

....

Directions: Pick a book to read. Then, fill out the form.

Title of book: _____

_____

Name of author: _____

_____

Name of illustrator: _____

_____

Characters in the book: _____

_____

Places in the book: _____

_____

The best part was: _____

_____

The best picture was: _____

_____

Book's rank (1 to 10): _____

Name: _____ Date: _____

Opposite Characters

Directions: Choose a book. Use words from the box to help you compare two characters.

animal or person big or little boy or girl	man or woman fast or slow good or bad

Character one	**Character one**
_____	_____
❶ _____	❶ _____
❷ _____	❷ _____
❸ _____	❸ _____
❹ _____	❹ _____

How are the characters the same?

_____

_____

_____

Once Is Not Enough—For Reading!

Directions: Try the ideas below to be a good reader.

- Skip words you don't know. Ask for help and get them right next time.

- Read in the characters' voices.

- Read in a loud or soft voice.

- Read like you are on the radio.

- Read and record the book. Play it for someone in your family.

- Read the book like a chant.

- Read in a silly voice.

- Read in a squeaky voice.

- Read the book to yourself. Then, tell it aloud.

- Choose music that goes with the book. Read it with the music.

Read It Again—And Have Fun!

Directions: Find a partner and try the ideas below to be a good reader.

- Read one page aloud. Have your partner read the next page.

- Choose characters. Read in the characters' voices.

- Read the book aloud together.

- Have one read the book while the other acts it out.

- Turn the book into a play. Add music.

- Have a good reader read part of the book. Then, read it the same way.

- Take turns making up new endings. Surprise each other.

- Read in opposites. One reads high, one low. One reads fast, one reads slow.

Name: _____ Date: _____

What Do You Think?

Directions: Fill out the form to show your opinion of a book.

Title of book: _Speak up_____

Author: _Miranda Paul_____

Illustrator: _Ebony Glenn_____

Topic of the book: _Speaking up_____

Setting: _School_____

Characters: _kids in classroom_____

_____

_____

What is the book about? _Speaking up when_
someone gets hurt, when someon
_says your name wrong._____

_____

What do you like about the book? _____
_Speaking up_____

_____

_____

Name: _____ Date: _____

Review Another Book

Directions: Fill out the form to show your opinion of a book.

Title of book: _____

Author: _____

Illustrator: _____

Topic of the book: _____

Setting: _____

Characters: _____

_____

_____

What is the best part in the book? _____

_____

_____

_____

What did you not like about the book? _____

_____

_____

_____

Name: _____ Date: _____

Why Did You Do That?

Directions: Choose one of the events from the list. Pretend you actually did it. Then, answer the questions.

> - Became a clown in the circus
> - Wore pajamas to school
> - Flew a plane to the North Pole

❶ What happened just before this event?

_____

_____

_____

❷ What were you thinking when you decided to do this? _____

_____

_____

❸ What happened during the event?

_____

_____

❹ Give a reason why you did it.

_____

_____

_____

#50884—Bright & Brainy: 1st Grade Practice

Name: _____ **Date:** _____

Ten Steps to the Facts!

Directions: Choose an informational book. Use the book to write a short report.

Step 1: Name of the topic: _____

Step 2: Name of the book: _____

Step 3: Name of the author: _____

Step 4: Important fact: _____

_____

Step 5: Important fact: _____

_____

Step 6: Important fact: _____

_____

Step 7: Write how this book is useful or not useful:

_____

_____

_____

Name: _____ Date: _____

My Worst Day

Directions: Read the story example. On a separate sheet of paper, write about a really bad day. Use words from the box.

Words for *the beginning*	Words for *the middle*	Words for *the end*
before	during	at last
early	next	finally

My Worst Baseball Day

When I woke up, I knew it was going to be a bad day. First, my pillow was under my feet. It was cloudy and gray outside. My hair was sticking up like a porcupine's. I smoothed it down with some gel. But, then I brushed my teeth with the gel. Yuck! And, I could not find my lucky hat. How could I play in the baseball game? Next, I found that my bike had a flat tire. So, I had to run to the game. Of course we lost, but at least I made a hit! It could have been worse!

Name: _____ Date: _____

Alien Day

Directions: Read the story example. On a separate sheet of paper, write about a really bad day. Use words from the box.

Words for *the beginning*	Words for *the middle*	Words for *the end*
before	during	at last
early	next	finally

The Day I Met the Alien

Before my alarm could go off, Pal was on my bed. He was barking like he'd seen a cat. At first, I thought he needed to go out. But, I was so wrong! Then, I saw why he was so upset. There was a tiny spaceship right on the table. It was right next to the box of cereal. While I reached for the phone, a small door on the spaceship opened up. Four robots raced to the cereal box. Next, they each grabbed a piece of toasted oats. Then, they raced back to the ship. At least my dog knows what happened.

Name: _____ Date: _____

Pack Your Bags!

Directions: On a separate sheet of paper, write a story about a trip. Use the words and questions to help plan your story.

Word Bank

adventure   airplane   airport   bus   car
cruise ship   hotel   map   meal   motel

- Where did you go?

- When did you go?

- Who went with you?

- How did you get there?

- What did you plan to see?

- What surprised you?

- What did you take?

- What did you forget to take?

- What did you buy?

- Would you go there again? Why or why not?

Name: _____ Date: _____

Step-by-Step

Directions: Read a how-to book. Then, answer the questions below.

1 What is the book's title? _____

_____

_____

2 Who is the author? _____

_____

_____

3 What is the book's topic? _____

_____

_____

4 What is the hardest step? _____

_____

_____

5 What is the easiest step? _____

_____

_____

Name: _____ Date: _____

How Do You Do That?

Directions: Choose something to explain from the list. Write the steps.

Things to Explain

- How to make a peanut butter and jelly sandwich
- How to wash a dog
- How to catch a fish
- How to train a dog to sit
- How to make pizza

Things you need to gather: _____

_____

_____

How to start: _____

_____

_____

Step 1: _____

_____

_____

Step 2: _____

_____

_____

Step 3: _____

_____

_____

How to finish: _____

_____

Name: _____ Date: _____

Dinner Time!

Directions: Plan a wacky meal for a book character.

Guests: Hansel, Gretel, Witch	
	Foods
Appetizer	chocolate-covered pretzels
Bread	gingerbread
Soup	cherry soup
Main Course	chicken fingers
	sweet potato fries
	carrot sticks
Dessert	plum pudding
Beverages	root beer

Guests:	
	Foods
Appetizer	
Bread	
Soup	
Main Course	
Dessert	
Beverages	

Name: _____ **Date:** _____

Quick Writes

Directions: Try writing some of the ideas below to help you become a good writer.

- Newsletter

- Alphabet poem

- Food journal

- Restaurant review

- Letters between two characters

- Grocery list for a fairy tale character

- Dream

- Complaint to a book character

- Description of a favorite place

- How-to article

- Apology

- Horoscope or fortune

- Description of an imaginary friend

- Story written by your pet

Name: _____ Date: _____

More Quick Writes

Directions: Try writing some of the ideas below to help you become a good writer.

- Want ad for a job

- Ad for your invention

- Ad for a toy you want to sell

- Chant

- Bumper sticker

- Birth certificate for a fairy tale character

- Menu for a folk tale character's restaurant

- Tongue twister

- Life story of a pet

- Life story of an insect

- Weather report

- List of questions to interview a grandparent

- Description of a new game

- List of favorite books

- Description of your favorite stuffed toy

Name: _____ Date: _____

Partner Writing

Directions: It takes practice to become a good writer. Try these ideas with a partner.

- Writer 1 writes a sentence. Writer 2 writes the next sentence. Repeat.

- Writer 1 writes a question. Writer 2 writes the answer. Switch.

- Writer 1 writes the first line of a poem. Writer 2 writes the second line. Repeat.

- Writer 1 writes why he or she likes something. Writer 2 writes why he or she dislikes the same thing. Switch.

- Writer 1 writes about his or her best day. Writer 2 writes about his or her worst day. Switch.

- Writer 1 writes the beginning of a story. Writer 2 writes the middle of a story. Writer 3 writes the ending of a story.

- Writer 1 writes one opinion, such as why snakes make the best pets. Writer two writes a similar opinion, such as why mice make the best pets.

Name: _____ Date: _____

Listen Up!

Directions: It takes practice to be a good speaker and listener. Try playing these games.

Raise Your Hand

Select a leader. Have the leader choose a magic word that is used in a book. The leader then reads the book aloud. When other people hear the magic word, they should raise their hand.

Broken Telephone

Find five or more players. Sit in a circle. Have the first person whisper a sentence in the second person's ear so that others cannot hear it. That person whispers it in the next person's ear. Once the message has reached the last person, the person says it out loud. Often the message is not close to the original sentence.

Mime Time

Find two or more players. Have one player act out an action. You and the other players should describe what the player is doing. When a player has guessed what the action is, switch roles.

Name: _____ Date: _____

Listen to This!

Directions: It takes practice to be a good speaker and listener. Try playing these games.

What Am I?

Find five or more players. Write the names of different animals on sticky notes. Put the sticky notes on the players' backs. Have each player ask others questions about the animal, such as "Am I furry?" Keep asking the questions until the animal is guessed.

Number Fun

Find two or more players. Select a leader. Write the numbers 1 through 20 on cards. Mix the cards and put them on the table. Have the leader call out a number. The other players should try to find the number. The first person to get the card keeps it. The one with the most cards at the end wins.

Oops!

Find two or more players. Select a leader. Have the leader select a word. The leader then spells out the chosen word. The word can be spelled right or purposely spelled wrong. The other players should tell if the word is spelled right or wrong.

Name: _____ Date: _____

Count Up!

Directions: Write the missing numbers.

85	86	87	88	89
90	91	92	93	94
95	96	97	98	99
100	101	102	103	104
105	106	107	108	109

Name: _____ **Date:** _____

Count Higher!

Directions: Write the missing numbers.

90			93	
	96			99
		102		
105		107		
110				114

#50884—Bright & Brainy: 1st Grade Practice

Name: _____ Date: _____

Keep Counting!

Directions: Write the missing numbers.

95		97		99
	101			104
	106		108	
110			113	
	116		118	

Name: _____ Date: _____

Count Big Numbers

Directions: Count by ones from the first number.

103				
98				
116				
107				
86				

Name: _____ Date: _____

Be a Ten Detective!

Directions: Draw an *X* on each group of 10.

1

2

3

4

5

6

Name: _____ **Date:** _____

Lasso Those Tens!

Directions: Draw a circle around each group of 10.

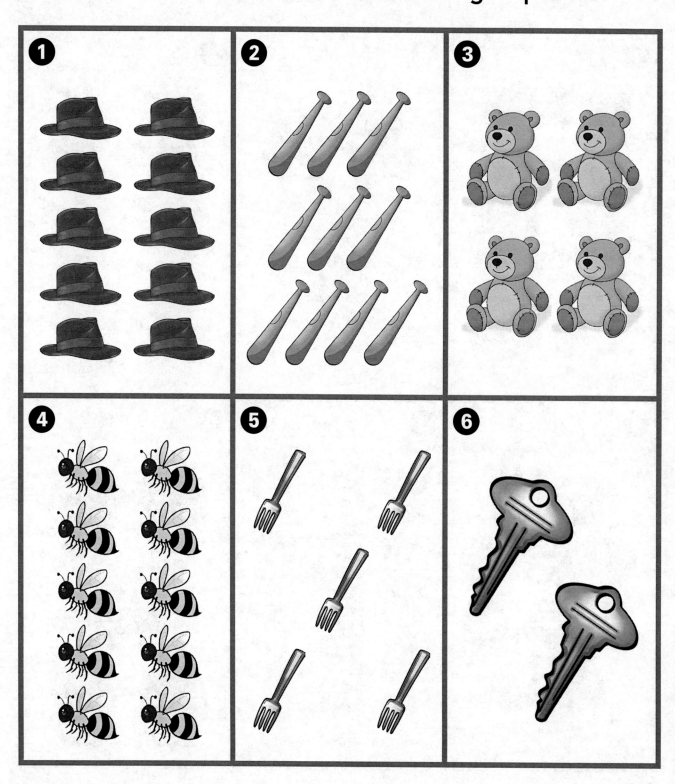

Name: _____ **Date:** _____

Domino Fun

Directions: Add dots so that each side has the right number of dots.

1

10   2

2

10   5

3

10   6

4

10   1

5

10   9

6

10   10

Name: _____ **Date:** _____

More Domino Fun

Directions: Add dots so that each side has the right number. Then, find the total.

 1

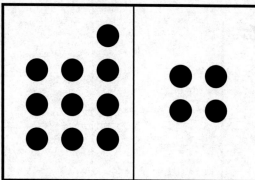

10 + 4 = ___14___

2

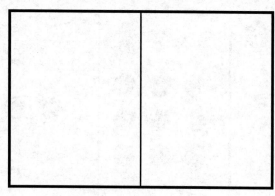

10 + 1 = _____

3

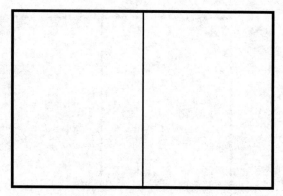

10 + 6 = _____

4

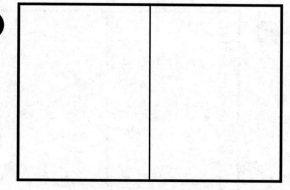

10 + 2 = _____

5

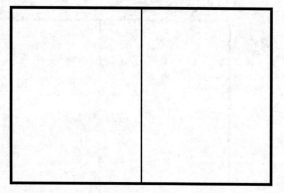

10 + 8 = _____

6

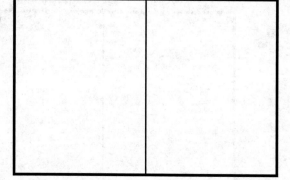

10 + 7 = _____

Name: _____ **Date:** _____

Finish the Dominos

Directions: Add dots so that each side has the right number. Then, find the total.

 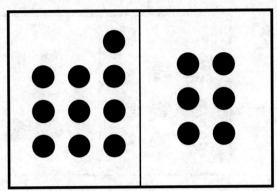

10 + __6__ = 16

 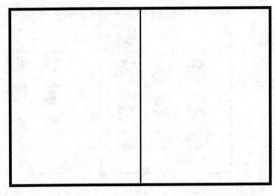

10 + _____ = 12

 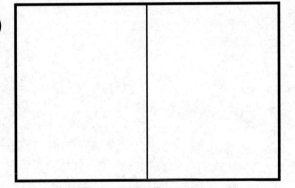

10 + _____ = 14

 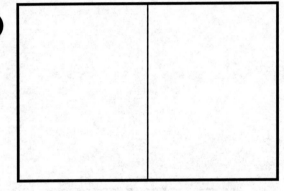

10 + _____ = 13

 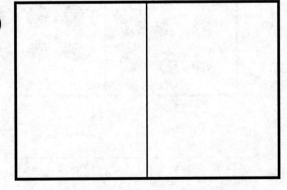

10 + _____ = 19

 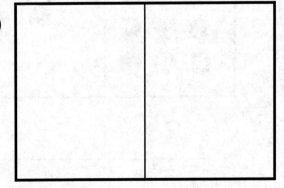

10 + _____ = 17

Name: _____ **Date:** _____

Find the Number

....

Directions: Write the number that is shown by the dots.

1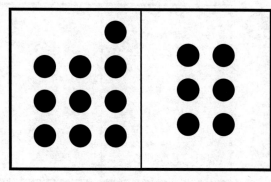

_____

2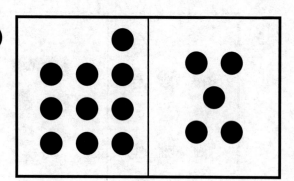

_____

3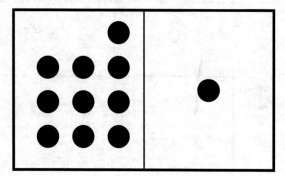

_____

4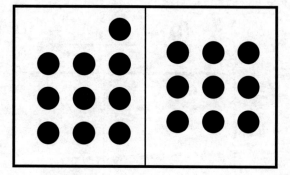

_____

#50884—Bright & Brainy: 1st Grade Practice

Name: _____ Date: _____

Split the Number

Directions: Tell how many tens and ones are in each.

 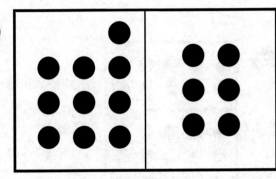

__1__ ten and __6__ ones

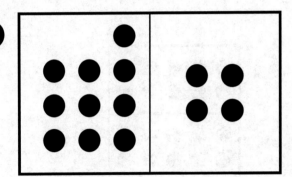

____ ten and ____ ones

 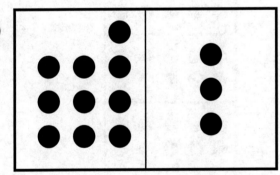

____ ten and ____ ones

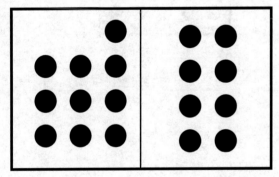

____ ten and ____ ones

#50884—Bright & Brainy: 1st Grade Practice

Name: _____ Date: _____

Stack the Dominos

Directions: Add up the tens for each set of dominos. Then, add the total.

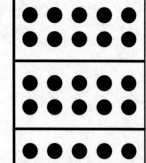

<u> 2 </u> tens= <u> 20 </u> dots

_____ tens = _____ dots

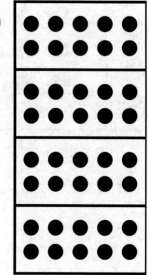

_____ tens = _____ dots

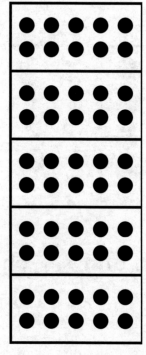

_____ tens = _____ dots

Name: _____ Date: _____

Tens Round-Up

Directions: Answer the questions.

1 How many tens are in the number 30?   ___3___

2 How many tens are in the number 80?   _____

3 How many tens are in the number 50?   _____

4 How many tens are in the number 20?   _____

5 How many tens are in the number 10?   _____

6 How many tens are in the number 40?   _____

7 How many tens are in the number 60?   _____

8 How many tens are in the number 70?   _____

9 How many tens are in the number 90?   _____

Name: _____ Date: _____

Ways to Say It

Directions: Answer the questions below.

1 What is 1 ten and 5 ones? _____15_____

2 What is 1 ten and 6 ones? _____

3 What is 1 ten and 1 one? _____

4 What is 1 ten and 4 ones? _____

5 What is 1 ten and 3 ones? _____

6 What is 1 ten and 9 ones? _____

Directions: Write how many tens and ones each number has.

7 14 = _____1_____ ten and _____4_____ ones

8 17 = _____ ten and _____ ones

9 13 = _____ ten and _____ ones

10 18 = _____ ten and _____ ones

Name: _____ Date: _____

One Way to Compare Numbers

14 is greater than 12.

That can be shown like this: 14 > 12

Directions: Write each problem in number form.
Then, write it in a sentence.

1 1 ten and 9 ones __19__   __19__ > __13__

1 ten and 3 ones __13__

2 1 ten and 7 ones _____   _____ > _____

1 ten and 5 ones _____

3 1 ten and 0 ones _____   _____ > _____

1 ten and 8 ones _____

4 1 ten and 1 one _____   _____ > _____

1 ten and 2 ones _____

5 1 ten and 6 ones _____   _____ > _____

1 ten and 3 ones _____

Name: _____ Date: _____

Another Way to Compare Numbers

12 is less than 14.

That can be shown like this: 12 < 14

Directions: Write each problem in number form. Then, write it in a sentence.

1 1 ten and 9 ones __19__   __13__ < __19__

    1 ten and 3 ones __13__

2 1 ten and 7 ones _____   _____ < _____

    1 ten and 5 ones _____

3 1 ten and 0 ones _____   _____ < _____

    1 ten and 8 ones _____

4 1 ten and 1 one _____   _____ < _____

    1 ten and 2 ones _____

5 1 ten and 6 ones _____   _____ < _____

    1 ten and 3 ones _____

Name: _____ **Date:** _____

Smaller, Greater, or Equal?

Directions: Decide which symbol should go between the numbers: less than <, greater than >, or equals =.

1 10 ____<____ 14

2 16 _____ 17

3 11 _____ 11

4 18 _____ 10

5 13 _____ 17

6 11 _____ 13

7 12 _____ 19

8 15 _____ 14

9 13 _____ 13

10 17 _____ 17

11 11 _____ 10

12 12 _____ 13

13 16 _____ 18

14 13 _____ 10

15 15 _____ 16

16 19 _____ 19

Name: _____ Date: _____

What Is One More or Less?

Directions: Choose a number for the answer that is just one more or one less.

1 13 < ___14___

2 15 > _____

3 14 < _____

4 18 > _____

5 15 < _____

6 13 > _____

7 19 < _____

8 14 > _____

9 12 < _____

10 16 > _____

11 17 < _____

12 19 > _____

13 16 < _____

14 17 > _____

15 18 < _____

16 10 < _____

Name: _____ **Date:** _____

What Is Equal to or One More or One Less?

Directions: Choose a number for the answer that is just one more or one less. If it has an equal sign, then the number should be the same.

1 12 < __13__

2 15 = _____

3 14 < _____

4 11 = _____

5 13 > _____

6 16 > _____

7 19 < _____

8 14 = _____

9 12 < _____

10 17 < _____

11 18 > _____

12 19 = _____

13 16 < _____

14 17 > _____

15 18 = _____

16 12 = _____

Name: _____ Date: _____

Count and Add

Directions: Use the number line to solve the problems.

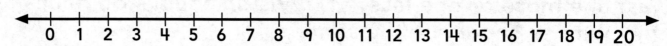

❶ Start on 6. Count forward 5.

What is the number? ____11____

❷ Start on 5. Count forward 10.

What is the number? _____

❸ Start on 8. Count forward 9.

What is the number? _____

❹ Start on 19. Count forward 0.

What is the number? _____

Directions: Use the number line to solve the problems.

❺ 9 + 2 11	**❻** 6 + 7	**❼** 10 + 4

Name: _____ Date: _____

Count and Add Bigger Numbers!

Directions: Use the number line to solve the problems.

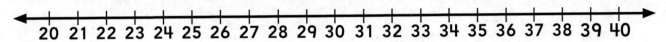

1 Start on 28. Count forward 6.

What is the number? ____34____

2 Start on 36. Count forward 4.

What is the number? _____

3 Start on 29. Count forward 9.

What is the number? _____

4 Start on 21. Count forward 12.

What is the number? _____

Directions: Use the number line to solve the problems.

5 21 + 8 29	**6** 37 + 2	**7** 30 + 7

Name: _____ **Date:** _____

Really Big Addition Problems!

Directions: Use the number line to solve the problems.

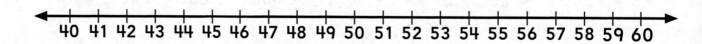

40 41 42 43 44 45 46 47 48 49 50 51 52 53 54 55 56 57 58 59 60

❶
```
  40
+  9
  49
```

❷
```
  46
+  2
```

❸
```
  52
+  7
```

❹
```
  40
+  7
```

❺
```
  41
+  3
```

❻
```
  43
+  6
```

❼
```
  41
+  5
```

❽
```
  50
+  4
```

❾
```
  51
+  6
```

#50884—Bright & Brainy: 1st Grade Practice © Shell Education

Name: _____ Date: _____

Add Them Up!

Directions: Use the number line to solve the problems.

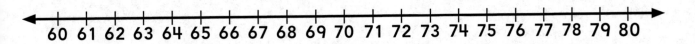

60 61 62 63 64 65 66 67 68 69 70 71 72 73 74 75 76 77 78 79 80

---

❶
```
  71
+  5
  76
```

❷
```
  74
+  3
```

❸
```
  77
+  2
```

---

❹
```
  79
+  0
```

❺
```
  70
+  4
```

❻
```
  76
+  3
```

---

❼
```
  62
+  2
```

❽
```
  68
+  1
```

❾
```
  64
+  4
```

Name: _____ Date: _____

Add Up More!

Directions: Use the number line to solve the problems.

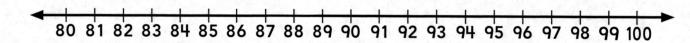

❶
$$\begin{array}{r} 91 \\ +5 \\ \hline 96 \end{array}$$

❷
$$\begin{array}{r} 95 \\ +4 \\ \hline \end{array}$$

❸
$$\begin{array}{r} 80 \\ +2 \\ \hline \end{array}$$

❹
$$\begin{array}{r} 98 \\ +0 \\ \hline \end{array}$$

❺
$$\begin{array}{r} 90 \\ +4 \\ \hline \end{array}$$

❻
$$\begin{array}{r} 81 \\ +4 \\ \hline \end{array}$$

❼
$$\begin{array}{r} 83 \\ +6 \\ \hline \end{array}$$

❽
$$\begin{array}{r} 99 \\ +0 \\ \hline \end{array}$$

❾
$$\begin{array}{r} 80 \\ +9 \\ \hline \end{array}$$

Name: _____ Date: _____

Can You Add These Tens?

Directions: Solve the problems.

❶
```
   10
+  10
-----
   20
```

❷
```
   20
+  10
-----
```

❸
```
   30
+  10
-----
```

❹
```
   40
+  10
-----
```

❺
```
   50
+  10
-----
```

❻
```
   60
+  10
-----
```

❼
```
   70
+  10
-----
```

❽
```
   80
+  10
-----
```

❾
```
   10
+  10
-----
```

Name: _____ Date: _____

Can You Add Tens and Ones?

Directions: Solve the problems.

❶	❷	❸
23 + 10 33	46 + 10	52 + 10

❹	❺	❻
68 + 10	34 + 10	71 + 10

❼	❽	❾
87 + 10	79 + 10	36 + 10

#50884—Bright & Brainy: 1st Grade Practice

© *Shell Education*

Name: _____ Date: _____

Can You Add More Tens and Ones?

Directions: Solve the problems.

1
```
   23
 + 36
 ____
   59
```

2
```
   46
 + 13
 ____
```

3
```
   52
 + 27
 ____
```

4
```
   68
 + 21
 ____
```

5
```
   44
 + 52
 ____
```

6
```
   81
 + 18
 ____
```

7
```
   82
 + 16
 ____
```

8
```
   29
 + 70
 ____
```

9
```
   36
 + 42
 ____
```

Name: _____ Date: _____

Even More Tens and Ones to Add

Directions: Solve the problems.

1
```
   66
+  13
   79
```

2
```
   56
+  13
```

3
```
   52
+  17
```

4
```
   58
+  41
```

5
```
   54
+  42
```

6
```
   71
+  18
```

7
```
   62
+  26
```

8
```
   38
+  60
```

9
```
   45
+  22
```

Name: _____ Date: _____

What Is 10 More?

Directions: Finish the chart by adding ten to each number.

Number		+10
1	10	20
2	15	_____
3	20	_____
4	25	_____
5	30	_____
6	35	_____
7	40	_____
8	45	_____
9	50	_____
10	55	_____
11	60	_____
12	65	_____

Name: _____ Date: _____

Find 10 More

Directions: Finish the chart by adding ten to each number.

Number		+10
1	13	23
2	26	
3	32	
4	78	
5	89	
6	57	
7	48	
8	37	
9	88	
10	74	
11	66	
12	47	

Name: _____ Date: _____

Take Away 10

Directions: There are 10 sticks per bundle. Solve each problem.

❶ Cross out 1 bundle.

How many are left?

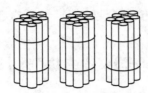

_____

❷ Cross out 1 bundle.

How many are left?

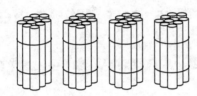

_____

❸ Cross out 1 bundle.

How many are left?

_____

❹ Cross out 1 bundle.

How many are left?

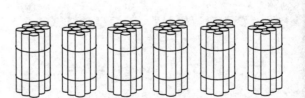

_____

Name: _____ **Date:** _____

Take Away 20

Directions: There are 10 sticks per bundle. Solve each problem.

❶ Cross out 2 bundles.

How many are left?

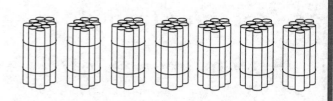

_____

❷ Cross out 2 bundles.

How many are left?

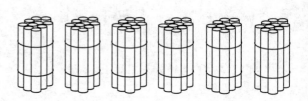

_____

❸ Cross out 2 bundles.

How many are left?

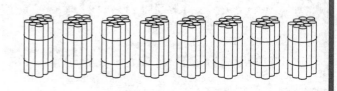

_____

❹ Cross out 2 bundles.

How many are left?

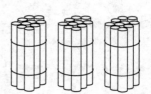

_____

Name: _____ **Date:** _____

Can You Subtract 10?

Directions: Solve the problems.

❶
```
   20
-  10
   10
```

❷
```
   30
-  10
```

❸
```
   40
-  10
```

❹
```
   50
-  10
```

❺
```
   60
-  10
```

❻
```
   70
-  10
```

❼
```
   80
-  10
```

❽
```
   90
-  10
```

❾
```
   10
-  10
```

Name: _____ **Date:** _____

More Subtraction of 10

Directions: Solve the problems.

1
$$\begin{array}{r} 23 \\ -\ 10 \\ \hline 13 \end{array}$$

2
$$\begin{array}{r} 26 \\ -\ 10 \\ \hline \end{array}$$

3
$$\begin{array}{r} 22 \\ -\ 10 \\ \hline \end{array}$$

4
$$\begin{array}{r} 25 \\ -\ 10 \\ \hline \end{array}$$

5
$$\begin{array}{r} 29 \\ -\ 10 \\ \hline \end{array}$$

6
$$\begin{array}{r} 28 \\ -\ 10 \\ \hline \end{array}$$

7
$$\begin{array}{r} 27 \\ -\ 10 \\ \hline \end{array}$$

8
$$\begin{array}{r} 46 \\ -\ 10 \\ \hline \end{array}$$

9
$$\begin{array}{r} 48 \\ -\ 10 \\ \hline \end{array}$$

Name: _____ Date: _____

Even More Subtraction of 10

Directions: Solve the problems.

❶
```
    12
 -  10
 ─────
     2
```

❷
```
    16
 -  10
 ─────
```

❸
```
    52
 -  10
 ─────
```

❹
```
    15
 -  10
 ─────
```

❺
```
    59
 -  10
 ─────
```

❻
```
    18
 -  10
 ─────
```

❼
```
    57
 -  10
 ─────
```

❽
```
    56
 -  10
 ─────
```

❾
```
    11
 -  10
 ─────
```

Name: _____ **Date:** _____

Keep Subtracting by 10

Directions: Solve the problems.

1 $\begin{array}{r} 92 \\ -\ 10 \\ \hline 82 \end{array}$	**2** $\begin{array}{r} 96 \\ -\ 10 \\ \hline \end{array}$	**3** $\begin{array}{r} 82 \\ -\ 10 \\ \hline \end{array}$
4 $\begin{array}{r} 95 \\ -\ 10 \\ \hline \end{array}$	**5** $\begin{array}{r} 99 \\ -\ 10 \\ \hline \end{array}$	**6** $\begin{array}{r} 88 \\ -\ 10 \\ \hline \end{array}$
7 $\begin{array}{r} 87 \\ -\ 10 \\ \hline \end{array}$	**8** $\begin{array}{r} 96 \\ -\ 10 \\ \hline \end{array}$	**9** $\begin{array}{r} 98 \\ -\ 10 \\ \hline \end{array}$

#50884—*Bright & Brainy: 1st Grade Practice*

Name: _____ Date: _____

Addition Word Problems

Directions: Write the numbers to make an addition problem. Then, write the answer below each problem.

1 Duke has 5 dog bones. Kim gave him 3 more. How many does he have now?

___5___ + ___3___ = ___8___ dog bones

2 Fluffy has 3 catnip toys. Sam gave her 2 more. How many does she have now?

___3___ + ___2___ = ___5___ catnip toys

3 Jack has 5 stickers. His dad gave him 6 more. How many does he have now?

___5___ + ___6___ = ___11___ stickers

4 Mom has 8 hats. Sue gave her 3 more. How many does she have now?

___8___ + ___3___ = ___11___ hats

Name: _____ Date: _____

More Addition Word Problems

Directions: Write the numbers to make an addition problem. Then, write the answer below each problem.

1 There are 6 frogs in the pond. Then, 6 more came. How many frogs are in the pond?

_____ + _____ = _____ frogs

2 There are 2 ponies on the farm. The farmer bought 3 more. How many ponies are on the farm?

_____ + _____ = _____ ponies

3 Lela has 13 quarters. Her dad gave her 2 more. How many quarters does Lela have now?

_____ + _____ = _____ quarters

4 Mona has 16 pairs of shoes. Her mom gave her 1 more. How many pairs of shoes does she have now?

_____ + _____ = _____ shoes

Name: _____ **Date:** _____

Subtraction Word Problems

Directions: Write the numbers to make a subtraction problem. Then, write the answer below each problem.

❶ There were 6 fish in the lake. A man caught 2. How many fish are left?

_____ – _____ = _____ fish

❷ Matt had 6 puppies. He gave 4 away. How many puppies are left?

_____ – _____ = _____ puppies

❸ Sofia had 3 quarters. She spent 1 of them. How many quarters does Sofia have left?

_____ – _____ = _____ quarters

❹ Andres had 12 marbles. He lost 4. How many marbles does Andres have left?

_____ – _____ = _____ marbles

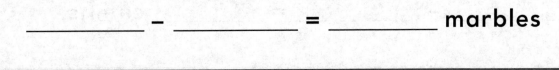

Name: _____ Date: _____

More Subtraction Word Problems

Directions: Write the numbers to make a subtraction problem. Then, write the answer below each problem.

1 Julia had 16 bows. She lost 10 bows. How many bows does she have left?

_____ – _____ = _____ bows

2 There were 11 ladybugs on a flower. The wind came and blew 1 away. How many ladybugs were left?

_____ – _____ = _____ ladybugs

3 Wendy had 13 dimes. She spent 5 of them. How many dimes does Wendy have left?

_____ – _____ = _____ dimes

4 Jim had 10 combs. He lost 3 of them. How many combs does Jim have left?

_____ – _____ = _____ combs

Name: _____ **Date:** _____

Picnic Time!

Directions: Draw pictures on the plates to solve the problem.

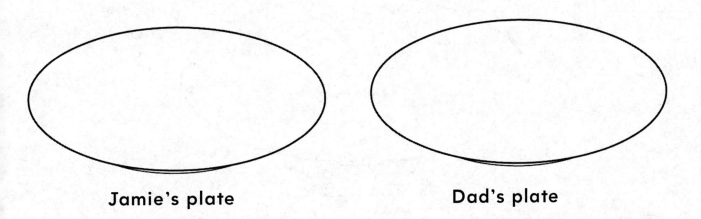

Jamie's plate   Dad's plate

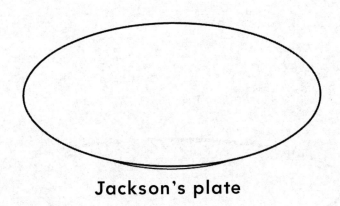

Jackson's plate

Jamie and Jackson went on a picnic with Dad. Dad put 2 hot dogs on Jamie's plate and 2 hot dogs on Jackson's plate. He put 1 hot dog on his own plate. Draw the hot dogs. How many hot dogs are on the 3 plates?

_____ hot dogs

Name: _____ **Date:** _____

Breakfast Time!

··

Directions: Draw pictures to solve the problems.

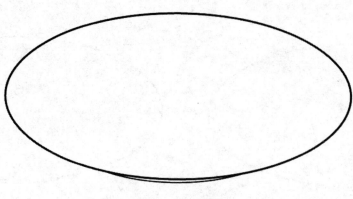

Tim's plate

❶ Tim put 2 pieces of toast, 3 slices of melon, and 2 fried eggs on his plate. How many items were on his plate? _____

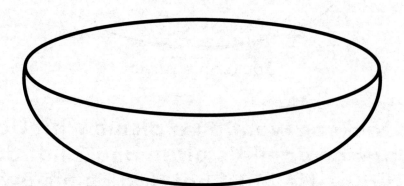

❷ Tim's baby sister had 8 pieces of cereal, 4 slices of banana, and 2 strawberries in her bowl. How many items were in her bowl? _____

Name: _____ Date: _____

Numbers in the Family

Directions: Make 2 addition and 2 subtraction problems for each family of numbers.

❶ 2, 16, 18

___2___ + ___16___ = ___18___

_____ + _____ = _____

___18___ − ___2___ = ___16___

_____ − _____ = _____

❷ 3, 15, 18

_____ + _____ = _____

_____ + _____ = _____

_____ − _____ = _____

_____ − _____ = _____

❸ 4, 14, 18

_____ + _____ = _____

_____ + _____ = _____

_____ − _____ = _____

_____ − _____ = _____

❹ 5, 13, 18

_____ + _____ = _____

_____ + _____ = _____

_____ − _____ = _____

_____ − _____ = _____

Name: _____ **Date:** _____

Questions About Numbers

Directions: Answer the questions.

---

❶ What number added to 6 makes 9? _____

_____ - _____ = _____

---

❷ What number added to 4 makes 8? _____

_____ - _____ = _____

---

❸ What number added to 3 makes 13? _____

_____ - _____ = _____

---

❹ What number added to 0 makes 16? _____

_____ - _____ = _____

Name: _____ Date: _____

More Questions About Numbers

Directions: Answer the questions.

❶ What number added to 6 makes 19? _____

_____ - _____ = _____

❷ What number added to 4 makes 15? _____

_____ - _____ = _____

❸ What number added to 3 makes 19? _____

_____ - _____ = _____

❹ What number added to 0 makes 17? _____

_____ - _____ = _____

Name: _____ **Date:** _____

Skip Forward

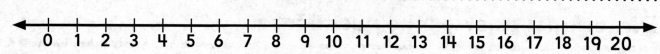

Directions: Solve the problems. Use the number line.

1 8 + 2 = __10__

2 1 + 2 = _____

3 4 + 2 = _____

4 10 + 2 = _____

5 6 + 2 = _____

6 11 + 2 = _____

7 14 + 2 = _____

8 12 + 2 = _____

9 18 + 2 = _____

10 16 + 2 = _____

11 5 + 2 = _____

12 3 + 2 = _____

Name: _____ **Date:** _____

Take Two Skips Forward

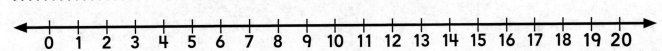

Directions: Solve the problems. Use the number line.

1 8 + 4 = ___12___

2 1 + 4 = _____

3 4 + 4 = _____

4 10 + 4 = _____

5 6 + 4 = _____

6 11 + 4 = _____

7 14 + 4 = _____

8 12 + 4 = _____

9 0 + 4 = _____

10 16 + 4 = _____

11 5 + 4 = _____

12 3 + 4 = _____

Name: _____ **Date:** _____

Skip Backwards

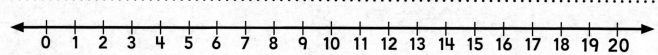

Directions: Solve the problems. Use the number line.

1 8 – 2 = ___6___

2 5 – 2 = _____

3 12 – 2 = _____

4 3 – 2 = _____

5 4 – 2 = _____

6 10 – 2 = _____

7 6 – 2 = _____

8 2 – 2 = _____

9 11 – 2 = _____

10 14 – 2 = _____

11 18 – 2 = _____

12 16 – 2 = _____

Name: _____ **Date:** _____

Take Two Skips Backwards

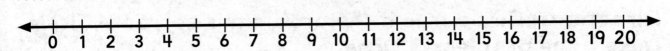

0 1 2 3 4 5 6 7 8 9 10 11 12 13 14 15 16 17 18 19 20

Directions: Solve the problems. Use the number line.

1 10 – 4 = __6__

2 5 – 4 = _____

3 17 – 4 = _____

4 20 – 4 = _____

5 4 – 4 = _____

6 13 – 4 = _____

7 6 – 4 = _____

8 12 – 4 = _____

9 11 – 4 = _____

10 14 – 4 = _____

11 18 – 4 = _____

12 16 – 4 = _____

Name: _____ Date: _____

True or False

Directions: Circle true if the problem is correct. Circle false if the problem is wrong.

❶ 3 + 4 = 4 + 3

3 + 4 = ___7___

4 + 3 = ___7___

(true)   false

❷ 2 + 4 = 3 + 3

2 + 4 = _____

3 + 3 = _____

true   false

❸ 5 + 1 = 1 + 4

5 + 1 = _____

1 + 4 = _____

true   false

❹ 3 + 4 = 5 + 1

3 + 4 = _____

5 + 1 = _____

true   false

❺ 2 + 2 = 3 + 1

2 + 2 = _____

3 + 1 = _____

true   false

❻ 7 + 1 = 3 + 4

7 + 1 = _____

3 + 4 = _____

true   false

Name: _____ Date: _____

Tricky True or False

Directions: Circle true if the problem is correct. Circle false if the problem is wrong.

1 $6 - 4 = 8 - 6$

$6 - 4 = \underline{\quad 2 \quad}$

$8 - 6 = \underline{\quad 2 \quad}$

(true)   false

2 $2 - 1 = 9 - 8$

$2 - 1 = \underline{\qquad}$

$9 - 8 = \underline{\qquad}$

true   false

3 $5 - 1 = 8 - 4$

$5 - 1 = \underline{\qquad}$

$8 - 4 = \underline{\qquad}$

true   false

4 $7 - 4 = 5 - 3$

$7 - 4 = \underline{\qquad}$

$5 - 3 = \underline{\qquad}$

true   false

5 $2 - 2 = 3 - 2$

$2 - 2 = \underline{\qquad}$

$3 - 2 = \underline{\qquad}$

true   false

6 $5 - 5 = 8 - 7$

$5 - 5 = \underline{\qquad}$

$8 - 7 = \underline{\qquad}$

true   false

Name: _____ **Date:** _____

Find the Missing Number!

Directions: Solve the problems.

❶ 4 + _____6_____ = 10

❷ 8 + _____ = 10

❸ 3 + _____ = 10

❹ 6 + _____ = 10

❺ 2 + _____ = 10

❻ 7 + _____ = 10

❼ 5 + _____ = 10

❽ 0 + _____ = 10

❾ 1 + _____ = 10

❿ 9 + _____ = 10

#50884—*Bright & Brainy: 1st Grade Practice*

Name: _____ Date: _____

What's That Number?

Directions: Solve the problems.

1 4 + ____9____ = 13

2 1 + _____ = 13

3 0 + _____ = 13

4 10 + _____ = 13

5 12 + _____ = 13

6 8 + _____ = 13

7 2 + _____ = 13

8 6 + _____ = 13

9 5 + _____ = 13

10 11 + _____ = 13

Name: _____ Date: _____

Measure Up!

Directions: Measure the things below.

Things to measure	Length
1 	\ —— pencil
2 	4 —— pencils
3 	l —— pencil

4 Which is the longest?  _____

Name: _____ Date: _____

Measure and Compare

Directions: Measure things with your index finger.
Have a friend measure the same things.

Things to measure	Length with my fingers	Length with my friend's fingers
1	_____ fingers	_____ fingers
2	_____ fingers	_____ fingers
3	_____ fingers	_____ fingers

Name: _____ Date: _____

Measure and Compare More

Directions: Measure the things below with paper clips.

Things to measure	Length with paper clips
1	_____ paper clips
2	_____ paper clips
3	_____ paper clips

4 Which is the longest? _____

5 Which is the shortest? _____

Name: _____ Date: _____

Measure and Compare Big Things

Directions: Measure these things with your hand.
Have a friend measure the same things.

Things to measure	Length with my hands	Length with my friend's hands
1 (lamp)	____ hands	____ hands
2 (dresser)	____ hands	____ hands
3 (bicycle)	____ hands	____ hands

4 Were your answers the same? _____

5 Which thing is the longest? _____

6 Which thing is the shortest? _____

Name: _____ **Date:** _____

Make a Clock

Directions: Make a clock by following the steps.

Materials
- paper plate
- construction paper
- paper fastener

1 Write the numbers 1–12 on the paper plate.

2 Mark the lines on the clock for minutes.

3 Cut the hour and minutes hands out of construction paper. Make sure the hour hand is shorter than the minute hand.

4 Poke a paper fastener through both clock hands and the center of the paper plate.

Name: _____ **Date:** _____

Write the Hour

Directions: Write the time for the clocks.

1

_____ : _____

2

_____ : _____

3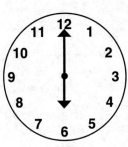

_____ : _____

4

_____ : _____

5

_____ : _____

6

_____ : _____

Name: _____ Date: _____

Write the Half Hour

Directions: Write the time for the clocks below.

1

_____ : _____

2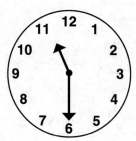

_____ : _____

3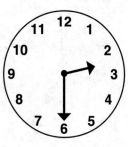

_____ : _____

4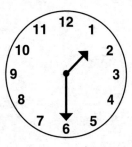

_____ : _____

5

_____ : _____

6

_____ : _____

Name: _____ Date: _____

Sort Them!

Directions: Answer the questions.

1 How many things to drink are shown? _____

2 How many things to eat are shown? _____

3 How many things to eat with are shown? _____

Name: _____ Date: _____

Sort Some More

Directions: Answer the questions.

1 How many things that move on land are shown?

_____

2 How many things that move in the air are shown?

_____

3 How many things that move in the water are shown? _____

Name: _____ Date: _____

Sort, Count, and Compare

Directions: Answer the questions.

❶ How many dogs are shown? _____

❷ How many cats are shown? _____

❸ How many more dogs than cats are shown?

_____

❹ How many insects are shown? _____

❺ How many more cats than insects are shown?

_____

217

Name: _____ Date: _____

Sort Them Out!

Directions: Follow the steps.

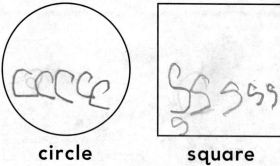

circle   square

1 Write 4 Cs in the circle.

2 Write 3 Ss in the square.

3 Write 5 Ts in the triangle.

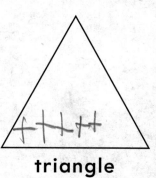

triangle

4 Which shape has the most letters? _____

5 Which shape has the least letters? _____

6 Add 3 more Ss to the square.

7 Add 1 more C to the circle.

8 Which shape now has the most letters?

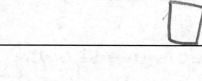

_____

#50884—Bright & Brainy: 1st Grade Practice

Name: _____ **Date:** _____

Shape Match

Directions: Draw a line from each shape to its name.

1

trapezoid

2

square

3

circle

4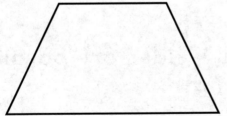

triangle

5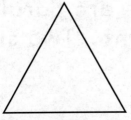

rectangle

Name: _____ Date: _____

Shape Riddles

....

Directions: Choose the answer or answers from these shapes.

circle   half circle   rectangle   square   trapezoid

1 We have 4 straight sides. Our sides are parallel.

We are a _____ and a _____.

2 I have 4 straight sides. Two are parallel. Two are not parallel.

I am a _____.

3 I am made of 1 line that curves. When you see me, you can't find where I begin or end.

I am a _____.

4 I have 1 line that curves and 1 line that is straight.

I am a _____.

5 I have 4 straight sides. All 4 sides are parallel. All 4 sides are the same length.

I am a _____.

6 I have 4 straight sides. All 4 sides are parallel. My sides are not all the same length. Two sides are longer.

I am a _____.

Name: _____ Date: _____

What Is Not True?

Directions: Cross out the sentences that are not true.
Hint: There could be two things that are not true.

❶
- I have a line that curves.
- I have a straight line.
- ~~I have a parallel side.~~

❷
- I have 4 sides.
- All 4 sides are parallel.
- I have a line that curves.
- Two sides are longer.
- Three sides are shorter.

❸
- I have 4 sides.
- All 4 sides are parallel.
- There are 2 sides that are longer.

❹
- I have parallel lines.
- I have a line that curves.

❺
- I have 3 sides.
- There are 2 sides that are parallel.

Name: _____ Date: _____

Shape Create

Directions: Read about each shape. Then, draw it.

1

I have 4 straight sides.

My sides are parallel.

They are the same length.

2

I am made of 1 line that curves.

I am round.

3

I have 3 straight sides.

4

I have 4 straight sides.

Two are parallel.

Two are not parallel.

5

I have 4 straight sides.

All 4 sides are parallel.

My sides are not all the same length.

Two sides are longer.

Name: _____ Date: _____

Make Shapes

Directions: Read the steps.

1 Cut out the shapes at the bottom.

2 Arrange two shapes to make a rectangle.

3 Arrange three shapes to make a trapezoid.

4 Arrange three shapes to make a square.

This page is intentionally blank.

Name: _____ Date: _____

Make More Shapes

Directions: Read the steps.

1 Cut out the shapes at the bottom.

2 Use 2 shapes to make a half circle.

3 Use 4 shapes to make a circle.

4 Use 4 shapes to make two half circles.

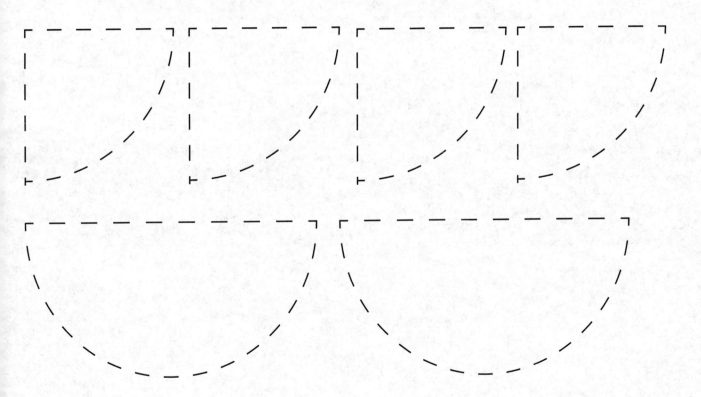

This page is intentionally blank.

Name: _____ Date: _____

Make the Pictures

Directions: Cut out the shapes. Put them together like the following shapes.

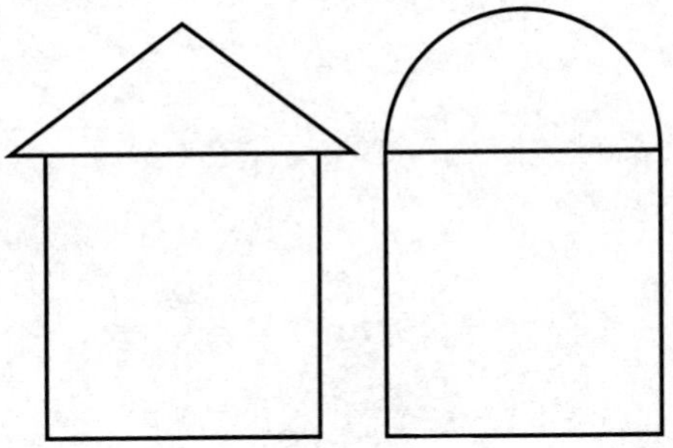

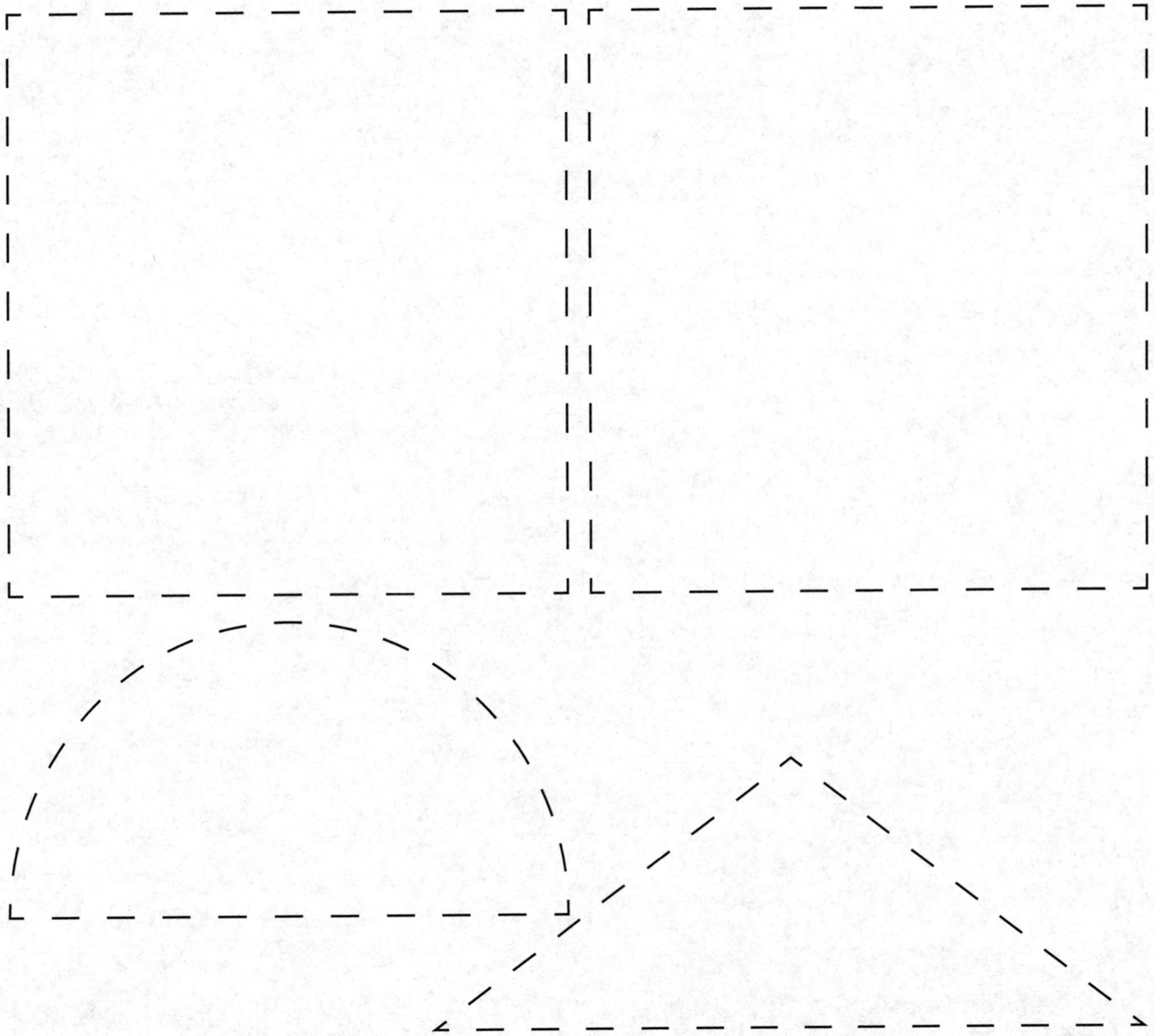

This page is intentionally blank.

Name: _____ Date: _____

Flat or Solid?

Directions: Answer the questions.

These figures are flat:	These figures are solid.
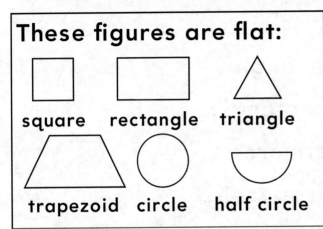	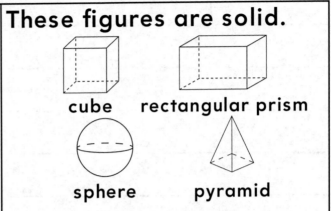

① How many sides does a square have? _____

② How many sides does a cube have? _____

③ How many sides does a rectangle have? _____

④ How many sides does a rectangular prism have? _____

⑤ Is a rectangular prism flat or solid? _____

⑥ How many sides does a triangle have? _____

⑦ How many sides does a pyramid have? _____

⑧ Is a pyramid flat or solid? _____

⑨ Is a sphere flat or solid? _____

⑩ How many sides does a trapezoid have? _____

Name: _____ Date: _____

How Many Shapes?

Directions: Write how many there are of each shape.

_____1_____ circle

_____ triangles

_____ rectangles

_____ squares

_____ trapezoids

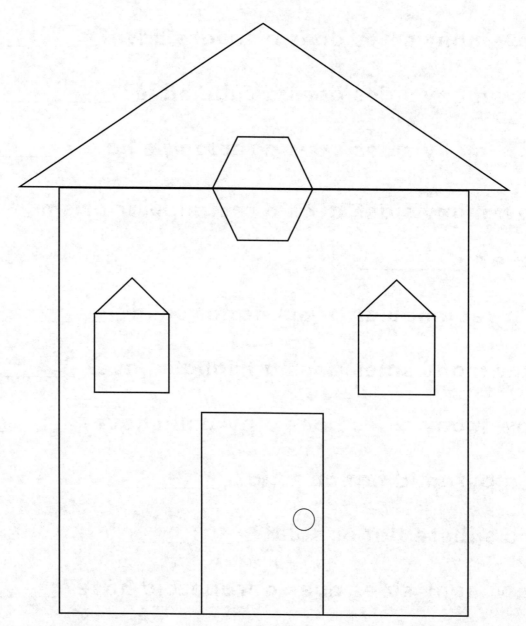

Name: _____ Date: _____

Divide These Shapes

Directions: Divide each shape in half. Choose the name for the halves from the Word Bank.

Word Bank

~~half circle~~

quarter circle

square

triangle

rectangle

1   ___half circle___

2   _____

3   _____

4   _____

5   _____

Name: _____ Date: _____

Color Shape Parts

Directions: Follow the steps.

❶ Divide the square in half. Color one half red.
Color the other half green.

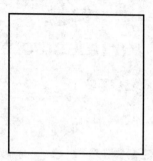

❷ Divide the rectangle in half. Color one half
orange. Color the other half yellow.

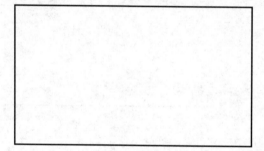

❸ Divide the circle in half. Color one half brown.
Color the other half pink.

Name: _____ Date: _____

Name the Shapes

Directions: Name the shaded portion of the shape.

Word Bank

half circle   quarter circle

square   triangle

1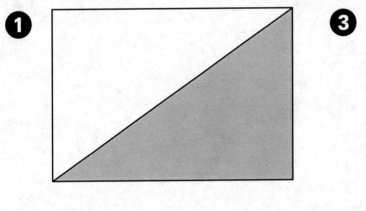

_____

3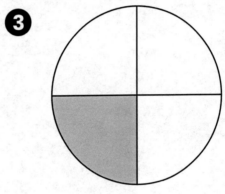

_____

2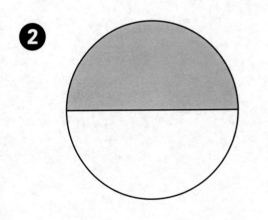

_____

4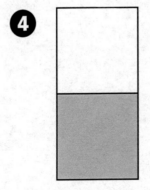

_____

References Cited

Annis, L.F., and Annis, D. B. 1987. *Does practice make perfect? The effects of repetition on student learning.* Paper presented at the annual meeting of the American Educational Research Association, Washington, DC.

Marzano, R. 2010. When practice makes perfect...sense. *Educational Leadership* (68):81–83.

National Governors Association Center for Best Practices and Council of Chief State School Officers. 2010. Common core standards. http://www.corestandards.org/the-standards.

Answer Key

Which Word Is Right? (page 11)
1. My
2. Do
3. I
4. There
5. Dad

Finish It! (page 12)
1. .
2. ?
3. .
4. .
5. !

Name That Sound (page 13)
Students should have circled the following images: pan, pot, cup, and bell.

Name More Sounds (page 14)
Students should have circled the following images: ant, bat, bed, and sun.

Pan or Pane? (page 15)
1. pan
2. van
3. Tim
4. mop
5. not

In the Tub or Tube (page 16)
1. tub
2. bit
3. slid
4. nap
5. cub

Find the Long Sounds (page 17)
Students should have circled the following images: queen, boat, and rain

More Long Sounds (page 18)
Students should have circled the following images: kite, leaf, goat, snail

Kit or Kite? (page 19)
1. kite
2. tape
3. robe
4. rode
5. slope

Hop or Hope? (page 20)
1. hope
2. ripe
3. pine
4. pile
5. made

Vowel Sound Match (page 21)
1. long
2. short
3. long
4. long
5. short

More Vowel Sound Matches (page 22)
1. Jan: short; Jane: long
2. plan: short; plane: long
3. note: long; not: short
4. pin: short; pine: long
5. pan: short; pane: long

Beginning to Blend (page 23)
br: brick, bread, broom, brush

dr: dresser, drum, dragon

gr: grapes, grass, grasshopper

Which Blend Is It? (page 24)
cr: cry, crab

pr: prince, pretzel

tr: train, trunk, truck, tree, triangle

Choose the Blend (page 25)
fr: fruit, frog

gl: glue, globe, glasses

fl: fly, flower, flag, flashlight

In the Blender (page 26)
pl: plate, plant, plane

bl: block, blueberries

cl: clock, cloud, clown

Blend Some More (page 27)
sk: skates, skunk, skirt

sp: spoon, spider, spaghetti

st: star, stool, strawberry

What Is That Short Vowel? (page 28)
1. a
2. a
3. o
4. i
5. e
6. u

Answer Key (cont.)

What Is That Long Vowel?
(page 29)
1. a
2. o
3. e
4. a
5. i
6. u

What Is That Final Sound?
(page 30)
1. w
2. l
3. n
4. g
5. x
6. f

More Final Sounds to Name
(page 31)
1. r
2. g
3. f
4. g
5. t
6. l

Ch or Sh? (page 32)
1. ch
2. sh
3. sh
4. ch
5. ch
6. sh

Tricky Beginning Sounds!
(page 33)
1. wh
2. wh
3. ph
4. th
5. th
6. wh

Tricky Ending Sounds!
(page 34)
1. ch
2. ch
3. ch
4. sh
5. ch
6. sh

More Tricky Ending Sounds!
(page 35)
1. ck
2. th
3. ck
4. th
5. ck
6. ck

What's That Word? (page 36)
1. desk
2. lamp
3. girl
4. vest
5. ring

What Are These Words?
(page 37)
1. duck
2. coat
3. map
4. hand
5. lock

Spell It Right (page 38)
1. coat
2. bee
3. hay
4. wig
5. tie
6. knee

Spell More Right (page 39)
1. boat
2. wheel
3. rain
4. goat
5. stool
6. horn

How Many Parts? (page 40)
1. circle u and e;
   2 syllables
2. circle a and e;
   2 syllables
3. circle i; 1 syllable
4. circle i and e;
   2 syllables
5. circle a, o, and e;
   3 syllables
6. circle i and o;
   2 syllables

How Many Parts in These
Words? (page 41)
1. circle a and o;
   2 syllables
2. circle a, a, and a;
   3 syllables
3. circle u, e, and a;
   3 syllables
4. circle o;
   1 syllable
5. circle u and e;
   2 syllables
6. circle u;
   1 syllable

Answer Key (cont.)

How Many Syllables?
(page 42)

1. circle e and y;
   2 syllables
2. circle a and o;
   2 syllables
3. circle i and e;
   2 syllables
4. circle a and a;
   2 syllables
5. circle i and y;
   2 syllables
6. circle i and e;
   2 syllables

Read Longer Words
(page 43)

1. mitten
2. ladder
3. flower
4. lemon
5. rabbit

Read More Longer Words
(page 44)

1. pizza
2. triangle
3. umbrella
4. carrot
5. dragon

Learn About Endings
(page 45)

1. safely
2. softly
3. sadly
4. loudly
5. quickly

Learn About More Endings
(page 46)

1. thanking
2. helping
3. playing
4. singing
5. looking

Read These Instant Words
(page 47)

1. These
2. There
3. This
4. These
5. There

Read More Instant Words
(page 48)

1. Where
2. We
3. Who
4. We
5. What

Read Even More Instant
Words (page 49)

1. said
2. saw
3. some
4. was
5. was

Print These Letters
(page 50)

Students should have
properly traced uppercase
and lowercase letters.

Print More Letters (page 51)

Students should have
properly traced uppercase
and lowercase letters.

Print Even More Letters
(page 52)

Students should have
properly traced uppercase
and lowercase letters.

Still More Letters (page 53)

Students should have
properly traced uppercase
and lowercase letters.

Name These Nouns
(page 54)

1. mother, father, child,
   baby, aunt, girl, boy
2. house, farm, school, zoo,
   town
3. drum, rope, boat, pan,
   lid, box
4. sadness, happiness,
   surprise, anger

Naming More Nouns
(page 55)

1. b should be shaded
2. n should be shaded
3. v should be shaded
4. r should be shaded
5. i should be shaded
6. q should be shaded
7. b should be shaded
8. p should be shaded
9. l should be shaded

Answer: a mushroom

Answer Key *(cont.)*

Show Ownership (page 56)
1. 's
2. 's
3. 's
4. 's
5. 's

1. the dog's bone
2. the boy's pig
3. Jose's bike
4. Lia's cap
5. Kai's box

More Than One? (page 57)
1. 1 dog, 2 dogs
2. 1 cat, 2 cats
3. 1 hen, 2 hens
4. 1 bed, 2 beds

Which Is Plural? (page 58)
1. Mom put three jars of jam on the table.
2. I need three sheets of paper.
3. My room has three windows.
4. It is just three days until my aunt comes.

Plural or Possessive? (page 59)
1. boys; boy's
2. cats; cat's
3. bird's; birds
4. pig's; pigs

Pronoun Play (page 60)
Circled: I, we, She, I, I, we, They, him, He, us, I, he, us, it

Pronouns at Work (page 61)
1. They went to the mall.
2. She got a new coat.
3. He wanted to look at the games.
4. Jose saw his friend. He waved at him.

More Pronouns at Work (page 62)
1. Anyone
2. Every
3. Everything
4. Nobody
5. All

Take Action! (page 63)
1. present
2. present
3. past
4. past

Words in Action (page 64)
1. future
2. present
3. future
4. present

More Words in Action (page 65)
1. past
2. future
3. past
4. present

Adjectives at Work (page 66)
1. *beautiful* should be circled with *sailboat* underlined
2. *big* and *cool* should be circled with *sail* and *wind* underlined
3. *hot* and *excited* should be circled with *sun* and *kids* underlined
4. *fast* and *blue* should be circled with *boat* and *water* underlined
5. *happy* should be circled with *kids* underlined

More Adjectives at Work (page 67)
1. fluffy
2. happy
3. huge
4. tall

Useful Adjectives (page 68)
1. bad
2. purple
3. some
4. striped
5. one

Put It Together (page 69)
1. or
2. and
3. and
4. and

Answer Key (cont.)

Combining Sentences (page 70)

1. Mom and Dad got us new clothes.
2. I had carrots and chicken for dinner.
3. I don't have a pencil or a pen.
4. Could I borrow your pencil and pen?

More Words to Combine (page 71)

1. because
2. and
3. but
4. or

Useful Little Words (page 72)

1. *the* should be circled with *dinner* underlined
2. *a* should be circled with *pot* underlined
3. *the* should be circled with *bread* underlined
4. *an* and *each* should be circled with *orange* and *salad* underlined
5. *the* should be circled with *plates* underlined

This and That (page 73)

1. *that* should be circled with *book* underlined
2. *this* should be circled with *book* underlined
3. *that* should be circled with *story* underlined
4. *this* should be circled with *book* underlined
5. *that* should be circled with *book* underlined

These and Those (page 74)

1. *these* should be circled with *clothes* underlined
2. *those* should be circled with *clothes* underlined
3. *Those* should be circled with *pants* underlined
4. *These* should be circled with *nights* underlined
5. *those* should be circled with *mittens* underlined

Preposition Play (page 75)

1. above
2. inside
3. under
4. behind

More Proposition Play (page 76)

1. in or on
2. to
3. on or in
4. beside
5. out

When, Where, Which Way? (page 77)

1. *in* should be circled; where
2. *down* should be circled; which way
3. *on* should be circled; where
4. *at* should be circled; where
5. *After* should be circled; when

Sentence Detective (page 78)

1. no
2. yes
3. no
4. no
5. yes

Ask a Question, Okay? (page 79)

1. Do you like apples?
2. What color is your bedroom?
3. How many dogs do you have?
4. How did you get to school?

What Kind of Sentence? (page 80)

1. I
2. D
3. I
4. D
5. D

Put These Together (page 81)

1. I like playing soccer, and I like watching soccer.
2. I went to bed, and I dreamed all night.
3. We packed up the car, and we left quickly.
4. Do you like dogs, or do you like cats?

Answer Key (cont.)

Find the Right Noun (page 82)
1. Ben; brother
2. Mom; hat
3. Dad
4. dog
5. Duke

Make Them Proper! (page 83)
1. January
2. Monday
3. February
4. no circle
5. Friday

Punctuation Station (page 84)
1. !
2. .
3. ?
4. .
5. !

More at the Punctuation Station (page 85)
1. .
2. .
3. !
4. ?
5. .
6. .
7. !
8. ?
9. .
10. !
11. ?

Punctuate and Capitalize (page 86)
capitalize: have, he, london, jumbo, for
1. ?
2. .
3. !
4. .
5. .
6. .
7. .
8. !

Commas in Lists (page 87)
1. I packed our hats, gloves, and socks.
2. Dad put our skis, poles, and helmets in the van.
3. We put in our skates, scarves, and goggles, too.
4. My mom brought out boots, sleds, and snow shoes.
5. We looked at the van. Where would we put snacks, drinks, and Fido?

Commas in Sentences (page 88)
1. Did you know that whales talk? Some whales click, and some whales sing.
2. Some whales seem to bark, but some seem to whistle.
3. Leave as is.
4. One whale makes some clicks, and then it stops.
5. Another whale makes clicks, and it stops, too.

Commas and More (page 89)
1. Mom was born on June 20, 1980.
2. My sister was born on June 20, 2011.
3. They were born 30 years apart! Isn't that funny?
4. My dad was born on July 4, 1980.
5. Boom! Dad says the fireworks are all for him.

Spelling Patterns (page 90)
1. boat
2. coat
3. rock
4. clock

More Spelling Patterns (page 91)
1. hair
2. chair
3. bee
4. feet

Text Fun (page 92)
1. forked tongue
2. long
3. The tongue helps it smell and know what's around it.
4. A Snake's Tongue

More Text Fun (page 93)
1. to clean its whiskers
2. stiff hairs
3. They are about as wide as the cat's head.
4. A Cat's Whiskers

Another Text (page 94)
1. you should be careful
2. wag its whole back end
3. ask the owner
4. A Dog's Tail

Answer Key *(cont.)*

Read This Text (page 95)
1. less than an inch long
2. six
3. leaves, fruits, and flowers
4. Stink Bugs

A Squirrel Story (page 96)
1. b
2. a
3. c
4. b

A Hedgehog Story (page 97)
1. b
2. a
3. a
4. b

Snurfers (page 98)
1. b
2. c
3. a
4. a

Rescue Dogs (page 99)
1. c
2. b
3. a
4. a

Using a Table of Contents (page 100)
1. b
2. b

More about Using a Table of Contents (page 101)
1. a
2. b

Picture Reading (page 102)
1. head, thorax, abdomen
2. 6
3. colonies

More Picture Reading (page 103)
1. 2
2. male
3. dig and fight

Another Text and Picture (page 104)
1. three to five
2. They sing.
3. Robins start their families in the spring.

One More Text and Picture (page 105)
1. Students' responses will vary. Possible responses include: trunk, leaves, branches
2. Students' responses will vary. Responses should include two of the following: keep the tree from falling over, take up nutrients, take water from the ground

Mice Are Nice (page 106)
1. Students' responses will vary. Possible responses include: they are cute, smart, easy to tame, clean, quiet, easy to feed.
2. They have short lives.
3. Student responses will vary.

The Best Invention (page 107)
1. Students' responses will vary. Possible responses include: they come in all sizes, are made for all ages, babies can ride in a trailer pulled by them, you can pedal with your hands or feet, they don't need gas, you can get exercise
2. They don't need gas and you can get exercise from them.
3. Student responses will vary.

What's That About (page 108)
1. image of person brushing their hair should be circled
2. image of a person ducking from a ball should be circled
3. image of a person bowling should be circled
4. image of a girl fanning her face should be circled
5. image of a soccer goalie blocking a ball should be circled

Answer Key (cont.)

What's That Mean? (page 109)

1. image of a girl skating should be circled
2. image of a boy fishing should be circled
3. image of a boy tying his shoes should be circled
4. image of a boy petting a dog should be circled
5. image of a hand ringing a bell should be circled

Choose the Picture (page 110)

1. image of a man with a dog should be circled
2. image of a man watering plants should be circled
3. image of an officer and vehicles on a road should be circled
4. image of a pig in a pen should be circled
5. image of boys playing baseball should be circled

Prefix Match (page 111)

1. distrust—not trusted
2. displace—not in place
3. uncurl—not curled
4. unclear—not clear
5. unpack—not packed

More Prefix Match (page 112)

1. overstay—to be somewhere too long
2. underage—to be too young
3. overtired—to be worn out
4. overcoat—an outer jacket or coat
5. undersized—to be too small

Suffix Choices (page 113)

1. biggest
2. slower
3. tallest
4. coldest

Work with Suffixes (page 114)

1. heaviest
2. funnier
3. silly
4. scarier

Suffix Match (page 115)

1. fearful—to be scared
2. endless—something that seems to never stop
3. helpful—to help out
4. painful—to hurt a lot
5. homeless—to have no place to live

Good Sports! (page 116)

Things in sports: baseball, basketball, football, ice skates, surfboard, skis, snowboard, soccer ball

People in sports: boxer, bowler, catcher, runner, surfer, skater, skier, swimmer

Good Work! (page 117)

Tools or things used at work: computer, desk, hammer, mop, paper, rake, ruler, saw

Workers: dancer, doctor, farmer, nurse, painter, pilot, teacher, writer

Buildings and Places (page 118)

Buildings: bus station, café, church, factory, fire station, house, library, school

Places: city, country, field, neighborhood, park, seaport, town, village

Taking Action or Having Feelings? (page 119)

Emotions or feelings: happiness, joy, afraid, sorrow, thankful, thrilled, worried, scared

Actions: find, give, help, clap, play, share, start, take, work

Answer Key _(cont.)

What Does It Mean? (page 120)

Student responses will vary. Responses include:

1. animal; furry
2. insect; tiny
3. animal; wild
4. person; crawls
5. vehicle; big

Tell All About It! (page 121)

Student responses will vary. Possible responses include:

1. food; red
2. food; white
3. vehicle; red
4. person; female
5. plant; green

Make the Connection! (page 122)

1. bedroom, library, home
2. park, street
3. garage, home, park, street, yard
4. park, yard
5. bedroom, garage, home, park, street, yard, bedroom

Where Might It Be? (page 123)

1. zoo, mountains, river
2. mountains, park, river, store, street, yard, zoo
3. park, yard
4. mountains, park, river, street, yard, zoo
5. mountains, park, store, street, river, yard, zoo

Meaning Match! (page 124)

1. question
2. amaze
3. begin
4. shout
5. speak

Noun Match! (page 125)

1. auto
2. present
3. work
4. trash
5. pair

Another Adjective! (page 126)

1. aged
2. flat
3. grand
4. tiny
5. glad

Meaning Magic! (page 127)

1. near
2. fat
3. all
4. bother
5. end

The Frogs Who Wanted a King (pages 128–129)

1. b
2. c
3. a
4. c

The Fox, the Rooster, and the Dog (pages 130–131)

1. c
2. a
3. a
4. b
5. Students' responses will vary.

The Wind or the Sun? (pages 132–133)

1. b
2. c
3. a
4. b
5. Students' responses will vary.

The Grasshopper and the Ant (pages 134–135)

1. a
2. c
3. b
4. c
5. Students' responses will vary.

Book Log (page 136)

Students' responses will vary.

Opposite Characters (page 137)

Students' responses will vary.

What Do You Think? (page 140)

Students' responses will vary.

Review Another Book (page 141)

Students' responses will vary.

Why Did You Do That? (page 142)

Students' responses will vary.

Answer Key (cont.)

**Ten Steps to the Facts!
(page 143)**

Students' responses will vary.

My Worst Day (page 144)

Students' responses will vary.

Alien Day (page 145)

Students' responses will vary.

Pack Your Bags! (page 146)

Students' responses will vary.

Step-by-Step (page 147)

Students' responses will vary.

**How Do You Do That?
(page 148)**

Students' responses will vary.

Dinner Time! (page 149)

Students' responses will vary.

Quick Writes (page 150)

Students' responses will vary.

**More Quick Writes
(page 151)**

Students' responses will vary.

Partner Writing (page 152)

Students' responses will vary.

Listen Up! (page 153)

Students' responses will vary.

Listen to This! (page 154)

Students' responses will vary.

Count Up! (page 155)

86, 88, 89, 91, 92, 94, 95, 98, 99, 101, 102, 103, 105, 106, 107, 108

Count Higher! (page 156)

91, 92, 94, 95, 97, 98, 100, 101, 103, 104, 106, 108, 109, 111, 112, 113

Keep Counting! (page 157)

96, 98, 100, 102, 103, 105, 107, 109, 111, 112, 114, 115, 117, 119

**Count Big Numbers
(page 158)**

1. 104, 105, 106, 107
2. 99, 100, 101, 102
3. 117, 118, 119, 120
4. 108, 109, 110, 111
5. 87, 88, 89, 90

**Be a Ten Detective!
(page 159)**

Boxes 1, 3, 4, and 5 should be crossed out.

**Lasso Those Tens!
(page 160)**

Boxes 1, 2, and 4 should be circled.

Domino Fun (page 161)

1. 10 dots, 2 dots
2. 10 dots, 5 dots
3. 10 dots, 6 dots
4. 10 dots, 1 dot
5. 10 dots, 9 dots
6. 10 dots, 10 dots

**More Domino Fun
(page 162)**

1. 10 dots, 4 dots; 14
2. 10 dots, 1 dot; 11
3. 10 dots, 6 dots; 16
4. 10 dots, 2 dots; 12
5. 10 dots, 8 dots; 18
6. 10 dots, 7 dots; 17

**Finish the Dominos
(page 163)**

1. 10 dots, 6 dots; 6
2. 10 dots, 2 dots; 2
3. 10 dots, 4 dots; 4
4. 10 dots, 3 dots; 3
5. 10 dots, 9 dots; 9
6. 10 dots, 7 dots; 7

Find the Number (page 164)

1. 16
2. 15
3. 11
4. 19

Split the Number (page 165)

1. 1; 6
2. 1; 4
3. 1; 3
4. 1; 8

**Stack the Dominos
(page 166)**

1. 2; 20
2. 3; 30
3. 4; 40
4. 5; 50

Answer Key *(cont.)*

Tens Round-Up (page 167)
1. 3
2. 8
3. 5
4. 2
5. 1
6. 4
7. 6
8. 7
9. 9

Ways to Say It (page 168)
1. 15
2. 16
3. 11
4. 14
5. 13
6. 19
7. 1 ten; 4 ones
8. 1 ten; 7 ones
9. 1 ten; 3 ones
10. 1 ten; 8 ones

One Way to Compare Numbers (page 169)
1. 19; 13; 19>13
2. 17; 15; 17>15
3. 10; 18; 18>10
4. 11; 12; 12>11
5. 16; 13; 16>13

Another Way to Compare Numbers (page 170)
1. 19; 13; 13<19
2. 17; 15; 15<17
3. 10; 18; 10<18
4. 11; 12; 11<12
5. 16; 13; 13<16

Smaller, Greater, or Equal? (page 171)
1. <
2. <
3. =
4. >
5. <
6. <
7. <
8. >
9. =
10. =
11. >
12. <
13. <
14. >
15. <
16. =

What Is One More or Less? (page 172)
1. 14
2. 14
3. 15
4. 17
5. 16
6. 12
7. 20
8. 13
9. 13
10. 15
11. 18
12. 18
13. 17
14. 16
15. 19
16. =

What Is Equal to or One More or One Less? (page 173)
1. 13
2. 15
3. 15
4. 11
5. 12
6. 15
7. 20
8. 14
9. 13
10. 18
11. 17
12. 19
13. 17
14. 16
15. 18
16. 12

Answer Key (cont.)

Count and Add (page 174)
1. 11
2. 15
3. 17
4. 19
5. 11
6. 13
7. 14

Count and Add Bigger Numbers! (page 175)
1. 34
2. 40
3. 38
4. 33
5. 29
6. 39
7. 37

Really Big Addition Problems! (page 176)
1. 49
2. 48
3. 59
4. 47
5. 44
6. 49
7. 46
8. 54
9. 57

Add Them Up! (page 177)
1. 76
2. 77
3. 79
4. 79
5. 74
6. 79
7. 64
8. 69
9. 68

Add Up More! (page 178)
1. 96
2. 99
3. 82
4. 98
5. 94
6. 85
7. 89
8. 99
9. 89

Can You Add These Tens? (page 179)
1. 20
2. 30
3. 40
4. 50
5. 60
6. 70
7. 80
8. 90
9. 20

Can You Add Tens and Ones? (page 180)
1. 33
2. 56
3. 62
4. 78
5. 44
6. 81
7. 97
8. 89
9. 46

Can You Add More Tens and Ones? (page 181)
1. 59
2. 59
3. 79
4. 89
5. 96
6. 99
7. 98
8. 99
9. 78

Even More Tens and Ones to Add (page 182)
1. 79
2. 69
3. 69
4. 99
5. 96
6. 89
7. 88
8. 98
9. 67

What Is 10 More? (page 183)
1. 20
2. 25
3. 30
4. 35
5. 40
6. 45
7. 50
8. 55
9. 60
10. 65
11. 70
12. 75

#50884—Bright & Brainy: 1st Grade Practice

Answer Key (cont.)

Find 10 More (page 184)
1. 23
2. 36
3. 42
4. 88
5. 99
6. 67
7. 58
8. 47
9. 98
10. 84
11. 76
12. 57

Take Away 10 (page 185)
1. 20
2. 30
3. 10
4. 50

Take Away 20 (page 186)
1. 40
2. 50
3. 60
4. 10

Can You Subtract 10? (page 187)
1. 10
2. 20
3. 30
4. 40
5. 50
6. 60
7. 70
8. 80
9. 0

More Subtraction of 10 (page 188)
1. 13
2. 16
3. 12
4. 15
5. 19
6. 18
7. 17
8. 36
9. 38

Even More Subtraction of 10 (page 189)
1. 2
2. 6
3. 42
4. 5
5. 49
6. 8
7. 47
8. 46
9. 1

Keep Subtracting by 10 (page 190)
1. 82
2. 86
3. 72
4. 85
5. 89
6. 78
7. 77
8. 86
9. 88

Addition Word Problems (page 191)
1. $5 + 3 = 8$; 8 dog bones
2. $3 + 2 = 5$; 5 catnip toys
3. $5 + 6 = 11$; 11 stickers
4. $8 + 3 = 11$; 11 hats

More Addition Word Problems (page 192)
1. $6 + 6 = 12$; 12 frogs
2. $2 + 3 = 5$; 5 ponies
3. $13 + 2 = 15$; 15 quarters
4. $16 + 1 = 17$; 17 shoes

Subtraction Word Problems (page 193)
1. $6 - 2 = 4$; 4 fish
2. $6 - 4 = 2$; 2 puppies
3. $3 - 1 = 2$; 2 quarters
4. $12 - 4 = 8$; 8 marbles

More Subtraction Word Problems (page 194)
1. $16 - 10 = 6$; 6 bows
2. $11 - 1 = 10$; 10 ladybugs
3. $13 - 5 = 8$; 8 dimes
4. $10 - 3 = 7$; 7 combs

Picnic Time! (page 195)
1. 5

Breakfast Time! (page 196)
1. 7
2. 14

Numbers in the Family (page 197)
1. $2 + 16 = 18$; $16 + 2 = 18$; $18 - 2 = 16$; $18 - 16 = 2$
2. $3 + 15 = 18$; $15 + 3 = 18$; $18 - 3 = 15$; $18 - 15 = 3$
3. $4 + 14 = 18$; $14 + 4 = 18$; $18 - 14 = 4$; $18 - 4 = 14$
4. $5 + 13 = 18$; $13 + 5 = 18$; $18 - 5 = 13$; $18 - 13 = 5$

Answer Key (cont.)

Questions About Numbers (page 198)

1. 3; 9 − 6 = 3; 3 added to 6 makes 9
2. 4; 8 − 4 = 4; 4 added to 4 makes 8
3. 10; 13 − 3 = 10; 10 added to 3 makes 13
4. 16; 16 − 0 = 16; 16 added to 0 makes 16

More Questions About Numbers (page 199)

1. 13; 19 − 6 = 13; 13 added to 6 makes 19
2. 11; 15 − 4 = 11; 11 added to 4 makes 15
3. 16; 19 − 3 = 16; 16 added to 3 makes 19
4. 17; 17 − 0 = 17; 17 added to 0 makes 17

Skip Forward (page 200)

1. 10
2. 3
3. 6
4. 12
5. 8
6. 13
7. 16
8. 14
9. 20
10. 18
11. 7
12. 5

Take Two Skips Forward (page 201)

1. 12
2. 5
3. 8
4. 14
5. 10
6. 15
7. 18
8. 16
9. 4
10. 20
11. 9
12. 7

Skip Backwards (page 202)

1. 6
2. 3
3. 10
4. 1
5. 2
6. 8
7. 4
8. 0
9. 9
10. 12
11. 16
12. 14

Take Two Skips Backwards (page 203)

1. 6
2. 1
3. 13
4. 16
5. 0
6. 9
7. 2
8. 8
9. 7
10. 10
11. 14
12. 12

True or False (page 204)

1. true; 7; 7
2. true; 6; 6
3. false; 6; 5
4. false; 7; 6
5. true; 4; 4
6. false; 8; 7

Tricky True or False (page 205)

1. true; 2; 2
2. true; 1; 1
3. true; 4; 4
4. false; 3; 2
5. false; 0; 1
6. false; 0; 1

Answer Key (cont.)

Find the Missing Number! (page 206)

1. 6
2. 2
3. 7
4. 4
5. 8
6. 3
7. 5
8. 10
9. 9
10. 1

What's That Number? (page 207)

1. 9
2. 12
3. 13
4. 3
5. 1
6. 5
7. 11
8. 7
9. 8
10. 2

Measure Up! (page 208)

1. 1
2. 4
3. 1
4. Bat

Measure and Compare (page 209)

Students' responses will vary.

Measure and Compare More (page 210)

1. 5
2. 6
3. 4
4. newspaper
5. bear

Measure and Compare Big Things (page 211)

Students' responses will vary.

Make a Clock (page 212)

Students should have created a clock with the directions given.

Write the Hour (page 213)

1. 3:00
2. 1:00
3. 6:00
4. 5:00
5. 9:00
6. 10:00

Write the Half Hour (page 214)

1. 4:30
2. 11:30
3. 2:30
4. 9:30
5. 1:30
6. 6:30

Sort Them! (page 215)

1. 2
2. 3
3. 3

Sort Some More (page 216)

1. 3
2. 2
3. 2

Sort, Count, and Compare (page 217)

1. 4
2. 3
3. 1
4. 2
5. 1

Sort Them Out! (page 218)

1. 4 Cs should be drawn in the circle
2. 3 Ss should be drawn in the square
3. 5 Ts should be drawn in the triangle
4. triangle
5. circle
6. 6 Ss should be drawn in the square
7. 5 Cs should be drawn in the circle
8. square

Shape Match (page 219)

1. circle
2. square
3. rectangle
4. trapezoid
5. triangle

Shape Riddles (page 220)

1. square; rectangle
2. trapezoid
3. circle
4. half circle
5. square
6. rectangle

Answer Key (cont.)

What Is Not True? (page 221)

1. third sentence should be crossed out
2. third and fifth sentences should be crossed out
3. third sentence should be crossed out
4. first sentence should be crossed out
5. second sentence should be crossed out

Shape Create (page 222)

1. square
2. circle
3. triangle
4. trapezoid
5. rectangle

Make Shapes (page 223)

1. shapes should be cut out
2. rectangle should be made
3. trapezoid should be made
4. square should be made

Make More shapes (page 225)

1. shapes should be cut out
2. half circle should be made
3. circle should be made
4. two half circles should be made

Make the Pictures (page 227)

Shapes in the pictures should be created from the cut out shapes at the bottom.

Flat or Solid? (page 229)

1. 4
2. 6
3. 4
4. 6
5. solid
6. 3
7. 5
8. solid
9. solid
10. 4

How Many Shapes? (page 230)

1 circle; 3 triangles;
1 rectangles; 3 squares;
2 trapezoids

Divide These Shapes (page 231)

1. half circle
2. quarter circle
3. triangle
4. square
5. triangle

Color Shape Parts (page 232)

1. square should be half red and half green
2. half of the rectangle should be orange and the other half should be yellow
3. half of the circle should be pink and the other half should be brown

Name the Shapes (page 233)

1. triangle
2. half circle
3. quarter circle
4. square

Contents of the Resource CD

Contents of the Resource CD (cont.)

Contents of the Resource CD *(cont.)*

Notes

Notes

Notes